La Lettre volée à la Maison d'Érasme

Le Cabinet d'Érasme II - Hortus Erasmi

Scientific Committee

Daniel Abadie
Director of the Galerie nationale du Jeu de Paume, Paris

Michèle Antoine
Scientific assistant at the Institut Royal des Sciences Naturelles de Belgique

Françoise Aubry
Scientific assistant at the Institut Royal des Sciences Naturelles de Belgique

Christine Blanckaert-Lamoureux
Curator of the Horta Museum, Brussels

Mickey Boël

Annick de Ville
Project Co-ordinator
Brussels 2000, European City of Culture

Marie-Françoise Degembe
Director of the Parks and Gardens Committee, Province of Namur

Jean-Louis Godefroid
Director of Espace Photographique Contretype, Brussels

Érik Orsenna
of the Académie française

Baron Philippe Robert-Jones
Honorary Permanent Secretary of the Académie royale de Belgique

Daniel Vander Gucht
Sociologist (Université Libre de Bruxelles) and publisher

Cover : Jean-Paul Brohez, Summer 1999

Title page from *Rosa Gallica*
from Symphorien Champier, Paris, Jodocus
Badius, 8vo, 1518.

Cabinet d'Érasme II

HORTUS ERASMI

Compiled by
Alexandre Vanautgaerden

Making of the Garden

PROJECT MANAGEMENT
a.s.b.l. « Erasmus 2000 »

PROJECT CONCEPT
Alexandre Vanautgaerden, Curator

LANDSCAPE ARCHITECT
Benoît Fondu

ARTISTS (CONTRIBUTIONS TO THE GARDEN)
Catherine Beaugrand
Marie-Jo Lafontaine
Perejaume
Bob Verschueren

ARTISTS (CONTRIBUTIONS TO PUBLICATIONS)
Luc Claus
Bernard Gaube
Félix Hannaert
Aïda Kazarian

PHOTOGRAPHERS
Jean-Paul Brohez
André Jasinski

BANQUETS
Maryangela Gusmao

EDUCATIONAL SERVICES AND PUBLICITY
Kathleen Leys, Assistant Curator
Véronique Laheyne, Trainee
Vincianne Picalause, Trainee

GARDEN INFORMATION PANELS
Louise Van Geesberghen
Joël Van Audenhage

BOTANIST
Georges Mees

HORTICULTURAL MANAGEMENT
Plantation Service of Anderlecht Commune

ON-SITE WORK
Public Works Department of Anderlecht Commune

Making of the Book

AUTHORS
Michèle Antoine
Catherine Beaugrand
André Delvaux
Alexandre Vanautgaerden

PHOTOGRAPHIC CREDITS
Jean-Paul Brohez : cover 1, pp. 6, 8, 10, 11, 12A, 12B, 15A, 16, 20, 21, 22A, 22B, 27A, 28, 29A, 29B, 30B.
J.-B. Brohez & Homme et ville A.S.B.L. : p. 11.
Michel Clinckemaille : pp. 8, 9.
André Jasinski : 7, 10, 13A, 13C, 14A, 14B, 15B, 17, 29C, backcover
Paul Louis : p. 45.
Jacques Vilet : p. 27.
Alexandre Vanautgaerden : pp. 9, 30A, 31A, 31 , 31C, 31D.

EDITORIAL CO-ORDINATION
AND EDITORIAL OFFICE
Dahlia Mees
Marie Naudin (Trainee)

TRANSLATION
Désirée Schyns (Dutch)
Alain Van Dievoet (Latin)
Jacques Van Tongerlo
& Philip Gaskell, TranScanDirect (English)

ICONOGRAPHY
Eve Toubeau, Trainee
Aurélie Meeus, Trainee

GRAPHICS AND LAYOUT
[Sign'], Brussels

INTERNET SITE
Aurore de Decker
http://www.ciger.be/erasmus/

This publication has also appeared in French and Dutch language versions. It is accompanied by two other books about the Erasmus Garden: *Un premier jardin* and *L'homme qui tombait des étoiles*. Both will be published in the Autumn of 2002 by the same publisher.

Contents

The Man Who Fell from the Stars
Alexandre Vanautgaerden — page 7

More Haste, Less Speed
Alexandre Vanautgaerden — page 9

Of Words and Things
Michèle Antoine & Alexandre Vanautgaerden — page 11

The « Godly Feast »
Catherine Beaugrand — page 19

The Traveller *with a Map of the Garden*
André Delvaux & Alexandre Vanautgaerden — page 21

Among Friends Everything is Shared
Alexandre Vanautgaerden — page 27

Ars mecanica
Alexandre Vanautgaerden — page 32

Bibliography — page 44

Acknowledgements — page 46

DE HOMINE DE SIDERIBUS ORIUNDO
ALEXANDRE VANAUTGAERDEN

Ut communiter narratur, Erasmum Roterodamum primum vocatum esse sermone Belgico Geert. Postea prænomen suum Latine interpretasse Desiderium, quod significat cupitus. Vir litteratissimus, voluit quoque hoc prænomen in Græcum vertere, sed haud recte elegit nomen Erasmum potius quam Erasmium, verbum, quod originem trahit a verbo græcanico erasmio, id est percarus. Per totam suam vitam eius pænitebit hunc iuventutis errorem fecisse, partum inscientia Græci sermonis nec non studio inconsulto. Tantum anno 1506° apparet primo nomen totum Desiderius Erasmus Roterodamus (Cupitus, Percarus, a Roterodamo), cum iam quadraginta annos natus esset – in frontispicio secundæ editionis typographicæ Adagiorum editæ apud Iudocum Badium Lutetiæ Parisiorum. Desiderium, sermone Latino, etiam significare « de sideribus », ita ut nomen Desiderius modo magis poetico significet etiam : homo qui de sideribus descendit.

Adage 3144
SIDERA ADDERE CÆLO
Add stars to the sky

THE MAN WHO FELL FROM THE STARS. It is widely believed that Erasmus from Rotterdam's first Christian name was Geert, in Dutch. He later latinised his Christian name to Desiderius, i.e. the « Desired ». Being a good humanist, he decided to translate his Christian name into Greek, which he did imperfectly since he took the first name Erasmus (instead of Erasmius) which is derived from *Erasmios* (« the beloved »). Throughout his life he was to repent this error of youth due to his poor knowledge of Greek and his unconsidered enthusiasm. His full name Desiderius Erasmus Roterodamus (« the Desired, the beloved from Rotterdam ») appeared in print for the first time in 1506, when he was already forty years old, on the first page of the second typographical edition of the *Adagia* published by Josse Bade in Paris. Desiderius is also derived from the Latin *de sideribus*. So, Desiderius would mean more poetically : the man who fell from the stars.

Far Left: André Jasinski, *Plum tree (prunus cerasifera) in the « Garden of Maladies »*, Spring 1998.

Left: Jean-Paul Brohez, Summer 1999.

Festina lente
Alexandre Vanautgaerden

Hoc in capitulo tractabitur de suavitatibus hortorum mentis, de ratione in eis ambulandi, atque de civilitate eorum hortulanorum.

MORE HASTE, LESS SPEED.
The Erasmus House has delightful settings, as they were called in the Renaissance, that is to say a garden. We can hardly imagine today how it was in the summer of 1521, at the time of Erasmus' stay. In his twenty-two letters written in Anderlecht, he talked about his happiness at being there but never about the garden. Sometimes, far away from city pollution, he praised the quality of the air, which seems ridiculous to us today, and concluded his epistles with an *ex rure Anderlaco* (« from rural Anderlecht ») ; sometimes, speaking to the great French humanist Guillaume Budé, he informed him that, taking heed of his advice, he also had decided to « play farmer. »
¶ Erasmus gave no description of the garden. Does it mean he took no further interest in it ? He evidently did since we know his liking for philosophical walks and roses. However we have no image of the garden of his host, the canon Pierre Wijchmans : Erasmus did talk about it, he enjoyed it, in the evening, after riding from Brussels to Louvain without stopping, or in the afternoon when he welcomed a nuncio or some ambassador come to greet him.
¶ When he left Anderlecht in October, never to come back to the Netherlands, he began to dream of his own garden. Once he arrived in Basle at his printer's, Jean Froben, he was delighted to find a shady enclosure again. From that moment, attracted by this garden, he was haunted at night by dreams of paradise. He got up early to the song of night birds, prayed and then imagined an ideal garden which would provide the framework for one of his most beautiful texts, the *Convivium religiosum* (« The Godly Feast. ») This philosophical garden was certainly made up of all the gardens Erasmus visited and loved. He planted it with his nib and gardened it in the middle of the din made by Jean Froben's printing house presses, and with fingers not covered with moist earth but with ink. This paper garden was born in March 1522.
¶ During this *Godly Feast*, nine persons visited Eusebius' place. On the patio of the villa, they discovered a set of flower beds crossed by a little river with a fountain at its centre. Painted walls decorated the covered walks. Upstairs, there is a library flanked by a *museion* and a chapel. To the rear of the house, there is an area comprising a garden meant for women (a vegetable garden) and a garden for the head of the household (a medicinal-herb garden) placed side by side. Adjacent to the house, you find an aviary. The garden extends with, on the left, a wild meadow enclosed by a bramble hedge and, on the right, an orchard with a hive in the background. Also, at the end of the garden you find a house for people with contagious diseases but which, in the spirit of Erasmus, can also be converted into a perfect place for a dinner with friends. Everything in this garden (sculptures, adages, paintings) become pretexts for discussion.

Far left (above) : The « Garden of Maladies » laid out by René Pechère in 1987, Michel Clinckemaille, 1995.

Far left (bottom) : J.-P. Brohez, Winter 1999.

Left: Front façade of the Erasmus House Museum, M. Clinckemaille, 1995.

Below : Plan of the Garden of the « Godly Feast », A. Vanautgaerden.

Thee « Garden of Maladies » with a muse, J.-P. Brohez, Spring 2000.

Adage 2224
NUNC IPSA FLORET MUSA
The Muse herself bursts into flower

¶ The place is copiously provided with « philosophical rooms » whose purpose is to make visitors *humanior*, more human. ¶ The garden described by Erasmus is a philosophical garden very similar – at least in the imagination of Renaissance people – to the Ancient Lyceum. Philosophers have always known that gardens are places for the care of body and soul : Socrates under his plane tree, Aristotle surrounded by his disciples (the peripatetic : « those who love going for a walk and conversing ») or Epicurus... Strolling in a garden encourages solitude, study and friendly encounters : the road to oneself, to others, and to the world – must be travelled by walking, little by little, just as thought is constructed. ¶ Intimately linked with the tempo of the city, a garden is, as it were its happy double, and is enclosed in order to better underline and glorify this territory of childhood and desire. A place for the muses, a place for the spirit, a place for the body, the garden gives us this dialogue between art and nature : it is an open-air library where wind, warmth, and the passing of time have free play, making us better. It is a place where Nietzsche's terrible alternative is finally resolved : *liberi aut libri* (« childrens or books. »)

¶ Strolling, dreaming, observing, coming to a rest, this is the invitation sent to you by the « Philosophical Garden » of the Museum of the Erasmus House. The garden has a thousand faces and we want to reveal some of them to you in the following pages. However, others will certainly appear as you wander. As Eusebius told his friends and guests : « Far from being dumb, the whole of nature speaks and teaches a lot of things to the man contemplating it, if he pays attention and accepts being taught. » We have drawn up two walks, using words and maps. It is now up to you, dear visitor, to add other walks which will belong only to you and to your friends.

The focal point of the view along the pathway of Charles Van Elst (1932), A. Jasinski, Winter 1999.

DE REBUS AC VOCABULIS

MICHÈLE ANTOINE AND ALEXANDRE VANAUTGAERDEN

En capitulum in quo licebit candido ambulatori mente novas semitas perspicientiæ experiri. In quo etiam docemur quali ratione botanista hortum conclusum recluserit et effecerit ut philosophus quidam, doloribus corporis et ideo animi cruciatus, ex eo evasisset. Quomodo Aqua reiecerit in abyssum sempiternum adagia Magni Erasmi. Quomodo Sagittarius fontem Hermæ ex umbilico Vulcani exsiliendum curaverit. In quo narratur de Silva, de Arbore et de eius pomo cinerarii saporis, et quomodo quattuor climata Amicitiæ in eius structura delineata sint. Etiam de prodigio conclavis luminosi, quod præbet ei qui decipi vult donum duplicis visionis, et de miraculis pruni psychopompæ.

OF WORDS AND THINGS. Ancient Romans used the word *otium* to mean the happiness that is opposed to *negotium*, labour. They considered *otium* as man's capacity to do nothing, which made him free and at ease with himself and, therefore, with others. We have developed this « Philosophical Garden » for the *otium* of our visitors.

Otium, photography from the series « Vues de Liège », J.-P. Brohez, 1988.

Adage 4121
LIBER NON EST, QUI NON ALIQUANDO NIHIL AGIT
He is never free who never rests

¶ When you enter the garden, passing under the archway, your attention is caught straightaway by what lies before you. It is not a long distance view of nature, by rather one tamed by geometry. A path whose perspective ends with a Gothic sculpture under an archway stretches out before you in a green setting. Is it near ? Is it far ? Only your steps will be able to tell you as you go down the path laid out by Charles Van Elst, who made the first layout of the garden in 1932. Caught by the games that perspective plays, this path seems far away, very far away, and you feel the urge to jump over the first wall of the garden. But don't do it. ¶ On your left, you discover the medicinal-herb garden laid out

View along the pathway of Charles Van Elst (1932), J.-P. Brohez, Spring 2000.

by René Pechère in 1987. Here, squares dominate, but false squares, repeating similarities in differences and sizes: the eye enlarges the space. The landscape gardener was inspired by the background of the painting « The Justice of Emperor Otto », by Dirk Bouts in the XVth century and from the garden depicted in Erasmus' *Godly Feast*.

Adage 141
SERERE NE DUBITES
Do not hesitate to sow

¶ Hellebores, wormwoods, wild gingers, houseleeks, knotgrasses, figworts, celandines, daisies, mulleins... so many plants crowd the squares of this garden and correspond to headaches, tuberculosis, gout, sweats, gravel, osteoarthritis... During the whole of his life, Erasmus suffered the onslaughts of disease. He often mentioned his *corpusculum,* as he affectionately and cautiously, liked to call his « little body » shaken by sufferings. ¶ While reading Erasmus' correspondence again, we underlined every passage informing us of the plants he used to cure himself or those recommended by Paracelse or his other doctors. We do not diagnose Erasmus by using our contemporary knowledge. We therefore imagine his sufferings as he perceived them in order to build up a sensitive « botanical portrait » of the humanist. We leafed through many herbaria but what was finally planted is based on the work of the Mechelen doctor Rembert Dodoens, in his *Kruydtboeck* published in Dutch in Antwerp in 1554 and translated into French in 1557 by Charles de l'Ecluse. ¶ Look at the plants and trees before you leave the « Garden of Maladies » to enter the « Philosophical Garden » : you either choose, as you prefer, to go through the narrow door or pass under one of the basket-handle archways.

Above (top) : The « Garden of Maladies », J.-P. Brohez, Spring 2000.

Above : Verbena oficinalis, Vervain : headache, J.-P. Brohez, Summer 1999.

Right : Papaver Rhoeas, Poppy : headache, A. Jasinski, Spring 2000.

A leaf, A. Jasinski, Spring 1999.

¶ In the Garden of the *Godly Feast,* Erasmus told us that he : « studied there, or went [there] for a walk, alone or accompanied by a friend whom [he] conversed with. » Leaving a closed garden, you come into a second garden, made up, no longer of squares, but of flower beds in the shape of leaves imagined by the landscape architect Benoît Fondu. Each of them contains a botanical sample of the landscape crossed by Erasmus during his journeys. These leaves form many partial and independent territories, a summary of the world Erasmus knew, heterogeneous and deterritorialised pieces of nature brought together in the same place by the architect and four artists : Catherine Beaugrand, Marie-Jo Lafontaine, Perejaume and Bob Verschueren.

Adage 3317
TUAM IPSIUS TERRAM CALCA
Cultivate your own garden (Tend your own cabbage patch)

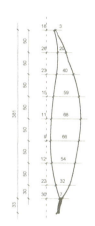

Study for flowerbeds in the form of a willow leaf, Benoît Fondu, October 1999.

Flowerbed 9 in the form of a lime tree leaf, Towards London : « Coastal Dune », A. Jasinski, Spring 2000.

¶ Among these leaf-shaped flower beds of willows, hornbeams, limes, and chestnuts, full of herbs and flowers, you find other leaves, made up of sky and water, born out of Marie-Jo Lafontaine's daydreams. Water flows endlessly in these oblong forms, just like the flow of life that nothing can hold back, not even by the memory of this current *Panta rhei,* « everything flows », Heraclitus used to say. Everything runs in a continuous and relentless rhythm which is only interrupted by the breath of the wind, the reflection of the moon, and the metamorphosis of clouds. If by chance, like Narcissus, you bend over these fountains to follow the play of the sky, sentences will appear, adages derived by Erasmus from ancient wisdom and folk culture. Reflected from the surface of the mirror of water, your image replies in a ceaseless dialogue.

Adage 464
QUID SI COELUM RUAT?
And if the heavens fell?

DIFFICILIA QUÆ PULCHRA
UBI BENE IBI PATRIA
AUT REGEM, AUT FATUUM NASCI OPORTERE
UBI AMICI, IBI OPES
CIVIS MUNDI SUM, COMMUNIS OMNIUM VEL PEREGRINUS MAGIS
SIDERA ADDERE CÆLO
FESTINA LENTE

The 7 adages in Marie-Jo Lafontaine's water mirror, typeset in Trajan.

Adage 1193
U BI BENE ,
IBI PATRIA
*Your homeland
is where
you feel good*

¶ Your course will almost inevitably bring you to the centre of the garden, to its point of equilibrium given concrete form in Bob Verschueren's observatory. This place is a focal point of Erasmus' philosophy of free will in the sense that it offers a view of both the fountain and of the medicinal-herb garden which leads to the museum entrance and of the spire of the collegiate church of St. Peter and St. Guidon : access to the spiritual (the spire, and in its continuation, the sky) through human works (the museum library). This place indicates the initiatory nature of the garden : to enter you must cross the unseen boundary.

¶ Bob Verschueren's creation draws its forces from the heart of the earth which is made of lava known by the poetic name of « moon rock ». In its centre there is a beech stump from which a thin trickle of water slowly invaded by moss flows out. Focal point of the garden, it is hollow to avoid blocking the view, and gives a power to the whole space without ever dominating. It is a minicosmos combining the elements, it is an invitation to humility and inner reflection. It is a space to withdraw to and from where the garden flows out. This inner retreat carries in itself the impulse to open to the outside, to others. Going from the source, the gaze rises, encounters the ground, discovers another garden and then rises to the sky. ¶ Let's move on. We have to go out and continue our journey across the garden.

Above :
View from Bob
Verschueren's
« Observatory »,
A. Jasinski, Spring 2000.

Bob Verschueren's
« Observatory »,
A. Jasinski, Spring 2000.

J.-P. Brohez, Summer 2000.

¶ The « Philosophical Garden » is surrounded by about a hundred trees, and these punctuate compositions of leaves with a vertical line. Being the links between the earth and the sky, they represent the elements circulating and the metaphysics of the space. Trees are mainly made up of air. When a tree burns, it goes back to the air. The fire given off is the sun's warmth, which has converted the air into a tree. Ashes represent the remaining part, that coming from the earth, and not from the air. ¶ In the centre of the garden, there is an orchard, rich in medlars, quinces, apple trees, cherry trees and plum trees. Taste the fruits but show respect for the tree and do not forget that greed, at the time of Erasmus, was one of the seven deadly sins.

Adage 3392
DULCE POMUM
CUM ABEST CUSTOS
How sweet is the fruit when its keeper is far away

Willow, A. Jasinski, Spring 2000.

Adage 2042
ALIENUM ARARE
FUNDUM
Cultivate another man's land

Adage 1
AMICORUM
COMMUNIA OMNIA
Among friends, everything is shared

¶ Catherine Beaugrand created a double work, a site dedicated to friendship and a series of paths composed of short lines which interact with other projects. These lines are represented by some *loci* (« places ») whose layout produces some kind of *genius loci* (« spirit of the place »). The garden is a map whose cardinal points should be incarnate and changing, depending on the route taken by visitors.

¶ If loneliness encourages meditation, company favours the curious discovery of what surrounds us and the people around us. What do we not share with our friends ? Catherine Beaugrand wanted to take the Erasmus adage seriously because she believed objects could speak and words existed through things. She reformulated Erasmus'adage in space by creating an enclosure of greenery (made up of beech trees) in conversation with a walnut tree. She created a space for relationship and intimacy where everything balances.

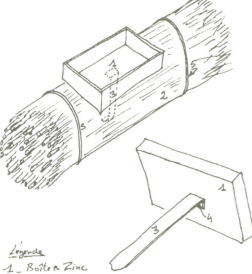

Studies by
Catherine Beaugrand,
October 1999.

Medlar tree,
J.-P. Brohez,
Summer 1999.

Study by Perejaume,
October 1999.

¶ Further on in the garden, a little apart from everything else, you find a room which represents the quarantine place described in the *Godly Feast*. Constructed from 11.500 glass lenses, this room is based on Perejaume's vision in order to attract our attention to the garden : it calls our perceptions into question. The garden is put to the test by this representation. ¶ As you enter, the overabundance of images gives you vertigo. You need to get a foothold and find your balance again. The sky - because the work has no roof - helps you to do so, with the clouds giving back unity and stability to the world. ¶ Outside this room of magic spells, everything is calm again. The room takes on its architecturally innocent appearance again. Our visitor, if he goes into the museum, will realise that this « room » has been designed according to the perspectives found in the museum's Renaissance gallery 1515 (the first example of the use of perspective in the southern Netherlands) and inspired by the coloured stained glass windows which filter the light. ❧

Adage 1248
HOMO BULLA
Man is a bubble

Adage 1234
GENEROSIORIS ARBORIS STATIM PLANTA CUM FRUCTU EST
A generous tree will bear both plant and fruit straightaway

The myrobalan plum tree (prunus cerasifera), A. Jasinski, Sring 2000.

¶ Walking along the wall of the "Garden of Maladies" once again, you find yourself face to face with the myrobalan plum tree. Half dead, half living, it resists time and men with doggedness. It is also very grateful to Jean Pierre Vanden Branden, former keeper of the Erasmus House Museum, for intervening on its behalf and allowing it to escape from being cut down when the garden was redesigned in 1987. This plum tree spreads its boughs over the medicinal-herb garden, and to good effect. Indeed, the medicine is linked to its name because in the 13th century « myrobalan » referred to several species of dried, flavoured fruits used for pharmaceutical preparations and included a play of word « mire » which meant doctor... ¶ Have a further look at the garden. It is still full of mysteries. No garden gives up all its secrets on the first visit. As you leave, think of your next visit. ❧

Adage 3286
NON SEMPER ERIT ÆSTAS
It will not always be summer

Portrait of Erasmus, Hans Holbein The Younger (?), ca. 1530, oil on wood, Erasmus House Museum, inv. n° MEH 80.

Convivium religiosum
Catherine Beaugrand

Ubi videre poterimus fabricam ac cogitationem unius ex artificibus huius horti philosophici nutritam scriptis Erasmi.

THE GODLY FEAST. The words « Philosophical Garden « conjure up the idea of a utopian place where you can spend time in contemplation and reflection. Is it possible to create such a place? ¶ In 'The Godly Feast' Erasmus recounts the story of a lunch party with some friends in a country-house. This text is original first of all in that the guests are not only asked to come with an appetite for food, but also with a thirst for knowledge. There is continuity, balance and there is a complementary nature in the dishes and drinks that are served out of the riches of the garden and the comments and discussions of the guests. In addition, it appears that the harmonious place where the meal is enjoyed, far away from the dangerous city, partakes of the conversation just as the appetites and aromas form part of the discussion. The garden is described in more detail during the course of two walks. The character of the garden reminds the guests, in both a solemn and light-hearted way, of the passing of the hours and seasons. From the moment that the guests enter the garden they are presented with an abundance of signs which they perceive in a variety of ways. The world presents itself as a world of smells, images and words, which create richly-variegated and graduated correlations. The meaning is never totally clear; there is no definitive interpretation of this unending dance of abstract and concrete. ¶ The objects speak. Words are present through things. 'I see Greek, but it does not see me', said Theophilus. Each time that we don't explain something simply, but rather expound about the matter, we are escaping into *enargia*. We then look at it as if it were printed in a coloured picture, and it looks as if we have made a painting rather than told a story or that the reader has observed rather than read. ¶ We can view « The Godly Feast « as a painting through which we walk. Houses and gardens are places where the perspective changes whenever the wanderer moves forward to point out new and unexpected meanings. Even by opening a window you get different viewpoints and different atmospheres, depending on the season. The movement of people connects the events that are scattered across the space. You could say that space is brought into being by discontinuity, moments of time and focal points. What is experienced during a walk around the enclosed garden you will find again in a journey across Europe. ¶ « I heard that you died in France; a couple of years later that you had returned from the land of shadows and were in Germany. Later again, I heard that you were being mourned in Germany, but that you had turned up in Italy. Finally I learned that you had died in England and that you now were on your way back to France from Avernus, the portals of the underworld. From an Italian you were seen to become a Frenchman, and from a Frenchman you became a German, a little as if when you see a bird come out of calf, and out of a bird some sort of corn (...) But from a poet you have been transformed into a theologian, only to take on the shape of a philosopher of the Cynic school; and for your final metamorphosis you have exchanged the Cynic for an orator... « Ambrosius Leo wrote to Erasmus. To this the humanist replied, « Through all these disturbances, Erasmus has remained Erasmus. « ¶ The idea of an individual adapting so energetically to circumstances while following his own never-ending search prompts us to ask what his vision was. Thus far, I have briefly indicated most of the ways in which the discourse can be changed while the thinking remains the same. This relationship between form and content, which is formulated in relationship to language in the above quotation, where he also refers to the fear of being confused by appearances, is emphasised as it might be in visual methods of representation. It seems that the subjective vision of space, seen and experienced, coincides exactly with the objective viewpoint that arises from the uniqueness of perspective: between journeying and vanishing point.

J.–P. Brohez, Winter 1999. / Right : J.–P. Brohez, Winter 1999.

Homo viator

André Delvaux and Alexandre Vanautgaerden

Ambulator noster considerabit hic tribulationes theologi humanistæ, quem inanitas fati in navem viatorum misit. Gaudebit etiam de terris mirabilibus et periculosis quas ille transiverit.

THE TRAVELLER. Erasmus was born in the northern part of the Burgundian Netherlands, in Rotterdam. He was a provincial who, through his work, managed to become a person who attracted the attention of the whole of Europe. At that time, the wealth was to be found in the south of the Netherlands, in the cities of Bruges, Louvain, or Brussels. His mother tongue was Dutch but the language he used everyday was Latin, which he spoke with an accent, Italians laughed at. A monk, priest, and poor man, he left the monastery of Steyn, near Gouda, in 1492 to begin his intellectual career to better his social position. Erasmus was a nomadic intellectual and his numerous trips were to convert him into the « Prince of Humanists » : the first great European. His life was linked with a river, with the waters of the Rhine. If we had to have just one picture of Erasmus, we should show him standing in front of his writing case or travelling by sea or on horseback - he was riding from Italy to England while he was writing *Praise of Folly*. ¶ Erasmus'constant travelling had a humanist basis because he was aware of the fact that the discovery of new horizons made man better by making him abandon his preconceptions. Just as we worked on his « body » in the « Garden of Maladies », we injected a geographical aspect to the garden in our choice of plants. Each (leaf-shaped) flower bed is made up from typical plants of the landscapes the humanist travelled through during his journeyings : plants discovered on the side of Brabantine roads, vegetation from coastal cliffs, meadow flowers... When you travel through this garden, following Erasmus' steps, you travel through the whole of Western Europe. The map of the garden will show you which paths to follow, from flower bed to flower bed, from region to region, from town to town.

Epistle 1314
CIVIS MUNDI SUM, COMMUNIS OMNIUM VEL PEREGRINUS MAGIS
I am a citizen of the world, my homeland is everywhere, or rather, I am a foreigner to everyone

> « *I took care of my health in Anderlecht, which is both a very famous place and also near Brussels, where you find the Emperor's Palace. (...) Almost every day I went to the city on horseback and (...) I also went back to Louvain without stopping. For many years – I give thanks to Christ – I have never been in better form than I was at that time* » (Letter to Marcus Laurinus, 1523).

¶ Erasmus stayed for five months in Anderlecht in 1521 and his stay was to be an important period in his life. After his stay he left the Netherlands, which had become a possession of the Hapsburgs, for Basle. He was never to return: the humanist's endless journey was coming to an end. He was beginning to age, being about fifty, and would only leave Basle when forced to by the arrival of the Reformation in 1529. In that year he took up residence in Freiburg-im-Breisgau.

Adage 3409
SAPIENS SUA BONA SECUM FERT
The wiseman carries his belongings with him

¶ A map of his journeys (p. 25) allows us to appreciate their geographical scope : an area which would be enclosed by two parallel straight lines drawn on the north and on the south of an axis connecting London and Naples and which, in reality, covered at that time practically all the most developed part of the known world, both from the economic and the intellectual point of view. Thus, all of his life, he was travelling through the heart of Europe. Just draw your own conclusions: from his birth (1467?) to 1492, Erasmus spent his early years in Holland ; from 1493 to 1499, he lived in France. However he never stayed in the same place for long periods of time : meanwhile he visited Holland and the southern Netherlands in 1494, 1496, 1498 ; he stayed there again for many months between 1500 and 1501. His first journey to England took place in 1499. He lived there from 1505 to 1506 and again from 1510 to 1514. From 1502 to 1504, he was in the southern Netherlands, in Louvain - he lived there from 1516 to 1521, but travelled to England in 1516 and 1517, Basle in 1518, Calais and Germany in 1520. Italy welcomed him from 1506 to 1509 : he visited Turin, Milan, Venice, Padua, Bologna, Florence, Naples, Rome, etc. He was in Switzerland for the first time in 1514, and stayed until the summer of 1516 – with journeys to London (1515), Brussels and Antwerp (1516). He lived in Basle a second time for a long period from 1521 to 1529 and finally from 1535 until his death in 1536. Between these two last stays, he lived in Freiburg - im - Breisgau in Germany, from 1530 and 1534.

Epistola 1342
NON UNIUS OPPIDI, CIVIS MUNDI SUM
I am a citizen of the world and not merely of a single country

¶ Erasmus travelled throughout his life driven by, as he wrote « his bad genius, which put him to the test with more adventures, more wanderings than those Neptune imposed on Homer's Ulysses. » (Letter to A. Léo, 1518.) Did he like travelling ? His writings remain ambiguous : he regularly complained about the discomfort of hostels and the dangers of the road but also ascribed a philosophical value to travelling. « Since we journey through the world, he wrote, we never have to be at rest. » ¶ Seasons put rhythm into his journeys because weather - warmth, rain, wind, snow and frost - exhaust travellers. After experiencing the severity of winter journeys, he decided to travel most of the time during spring or autumn.
¶ The high cost of journeys - the upkeep of a horse was almost as expensive as the traveller's personal costs - a day in a hostel was equal to the average wage of a harvester - was a source of constant worry for Erasmus. ¶ There were many reasons for these endless journeys: he was travelling because he had been invited by a patron or because he was looking for employment as a private teacher. He was sometimes following a patron, like the Bishop of Chambray whom Erasmus accompanied when visiting his diocese, or was on "active service" for the Emperor Charles V, to whom he was adviser, and whom he followed with the Imperial Court. The time in which he lived was not spared by war or by plague. As soon as they appeared, Erasmus left the region or city. He « had a change of scene » when he felt religious hostility towards himself, and he then deliberately distanced himself from Louvain Catholic theologians or German Protestants. He often travelled to visit some library or monastery where he hoped he could find some rare manuscript which he could consult, borrow, or purchase. Also, as his ultimate objective, he braved the discomfort of the roads because, anxious about the quality of the publishing of his works, he wanted to visit his printers : Froben in Basle, Bade in Paris, Manuce in Venice, Martens in Louvain or Antwerp. ¶ But, from the age of 25 he would also feel a deeper and constant need for exploration and discovery : he needed to see the world and meet people, to extend his knowledge and widen his circle of friends, deliver his humanist and Christian message. He certainly travelled so much because he had no family ties (he had been an orphan since the age of 12 or 13) and because his friends were his family. Erasmus was buoyed with the same state of mind as that which drove great navigators towards new lands at the other side of the sea, which were discovered the year he left his monastery in 1492: « to see and learn. »

J.-P. Brohez, Summer 1999.

HORTUS ERASMI 23

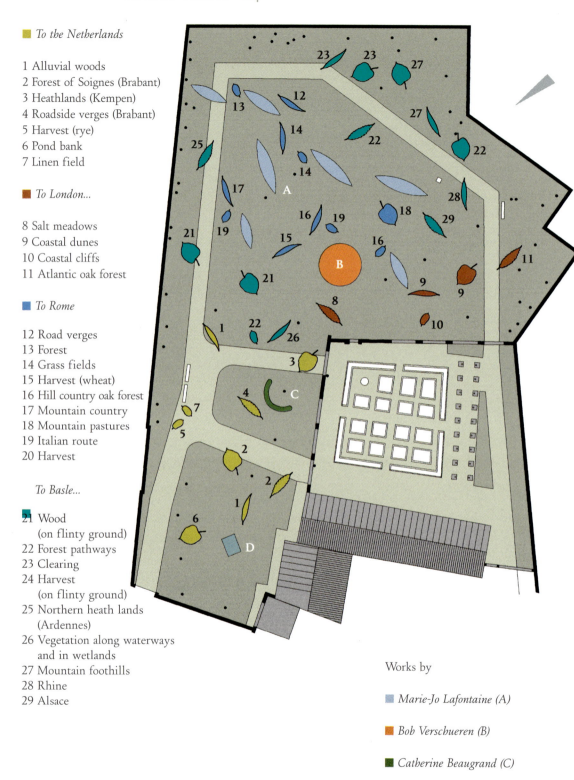

¶ We have given special prominence to four journeys which were important for Erasmus: within the Netherlands; towards London; towards Rome and towards Basle. For each of these journeys we have singled out the landscapes that Erasmus describes.

¶ In the Netherlands, in his youth, he lived in Rotterdam, Gouda, Deventer, Utrecht, and in 's Hertogenbosch. As counsellor to Charles v, after 1516, he regularly travelled up and down the southern Netherlands: Anderlecht, Antwerp, Bruges, Ghent, Mechelen and Brussels.

¶ When Erasmus left Paris to go to London, which he visited six times, he may have followed the following route: Paris - Clermont - Amiens - Calais/Boulogne - Dover - London - Oxford/Cambridge.

¶ In 1506–1509, Erasmus went on his « Grand tour » leaving London and crossing the Channel, he went via: Paris - Orleans - Bourges - Moulins - Lyons - Chambéry - Susa - Mont-Cenis - Novalese - Turin - Pavia - Milan - Bologna - Florence - Padua - Venice - Ferrara - Rome - Siena - Naples. He returned by: Milan - the Alpine passes - Chur - Constance - Strasbourg - Louvain - Antwerp - London - Cambridge.

¶ Three journeys to Basle are described in Erasmus' correspondence: the first in 1514, the second in 1518 and the last in 1521 (when he left Anderlecht and the Netherlands for the last time). He made the journey in both directions on the Rhine: Anderlecht - Mechelen - Louvain - Tirlemont - Düren - Andernach - Koblenz - Mainz - Worms - Speyer - Strasbourg - Sélestat - Colmar - Basle.

Amicorum communia omnia

Alexandre Vanautgaerden

Quomodo lectio « Convivii religiosi » servatorem Musarum duxerit ad rem botanicam, et quomodo inde nonnulla felicia colloquia de Artibus liberalibus et de harmonia sphærarum habita sint.

AMONG FRIENDS EVERYTHING IS SHARED.
The « Philosophical Garden » is the fourth garden to be laid out around the house in which Erasmus lived in Anderlecht. In the 16th century there was first an orchard and then, in 1932, the garden of the architect Charles Van Elst, which took the classical form of the goose-foot layout and finally, the garden of the landscape gardener René Pechère in 1987, which returned to the medieval structure of an enclosed garden. We found it was very important to maintain the memory of these successive gardens. That is the reason why I planned this philosophical garden as if it were one single stone of a much larger edifice. ¶ The starting point of this new garden is the culture of « Curiosity Cabinets » which, in the 16th century, combined places for the study of the sciences, the social sciences, and the fine arts. These cabinets were often composed of a library, a museum, and a botanical garden : they were taken as a model for designing the museum dedicated to Erasmus where paintings are displayed and books conserved and published, in the middle of a garden. ¶ I sketched out the project, which is being carried out today, in 1997 in the museum of Saint-Antoine l'Abbaye (Isère) in an exhibition entitled « Erasmus or the Praise of Curiosity in the Renaissance. » Books, works of art, animals, an anatomical model and even a garden were exhibited. This exhibition gave us the opportunity to meet, for the first time, one of the authors of the philosophical garden, the botanist Georges Mees, with whom we undertook this « adventure of the plants. » We tried together to let medicinal herbs speak. Thanks to his extraordinary knowledge of nature, we began putting together ideas and trees, books and leaves, by making a botanical portrait of Erasmus.

Adage 224
Ubi amici,
ibi opes
Your wealth is where your friends are

Left :
Ricinus Communis,
Castor oil plant : purgative,
J.-P. Brohez, Summer 1999.

Vignette :
Hans Holbein,
Erasmus in Gehäus,
wood-engraving by
Hans Luzelburger, 1535.

The « Erasmus Garden »,
Musée de Saint-Antoine
l'Abbaye,
Jacques Vilet, Summer 1997.

Adage 3681

QUOD PULCHRUM,
IDEM AMICUM

That which is beautiful is also friendly

¶ Under the famous portrait of the humanist painted by Holbein, his assistant Gilbert Cousin completed the engraving with a poem in which he informed us that we would not find the true image of the humanist in the work of Holbein, but in his writings. I took him at his word and tried to work, not with what we knew about the external appearance of Erasmus, through the works of his portrait painters, but through his texts and the way he said that he experienced the world ; portraying Erasmus according to Erasmus : *Erasmus ex Erasmo.* ¶ Just as the shape of a church represents the body of Christ, the garden of Saint-Antoine l'Abbaye was laid out following the plan of a basilica which became, in my opinion, the metaphor of the body of Erasmus. The medicinal herbs were planted at the places where disease and illness strike (medicinal herbs for treating migraines or fainting fits in the apse, at the head of the church ; herbs for treating osteoarthritis in the « arms of the transept », etc.) ¶ Our botanist friend was the first to get us to abandon our books in favour of going botanical, our hands in the soil, and our heads in the clouds. In the spring of 1998, we planted a hundred medicinal herbs in the museum's fifteen squares flower beds, trying to concentrate one single disease in each square, as we had done in Saint-Antoine. I have written « trying » because nature forced us to recognize our limitations and, from the very beginning, interfered with our nice organisation which we had been able to maintain at St Antoine l'Abbaye thanks to artificial lighting and daily care, sheltered from the wind and external influences. So, when we had planted around a hundred taxons, which are usually considered as « weeds », nature began to play tricks, with the help of butterflies and bees, sending us seedlings from many other « weeds » which were on our basic list (which contained around 450 species), but which fooled us and never landed in the right square! So, after one season we had understood that we had better abandon this rigid structure of one disease per square. Otherwise, we would have converted ourselves into « cleaning technicians », spending our time moving plants from square to square and cleaning up. ¶ While keeping up Pechère's garden, renamed the « Garden of Maladies », I could not help myself from looking over the fence towards the orchard and thinking of a text which had been haunting me since I had got involved in Erasmus studies : the *Godly Feast*, a text Erasmus wrote partly, it would seem, in Anderlecht or after he left the city with the memory of this garden he had so much appreciated during the summer of 1521.

The narrow gate between the « Garden of Maladies » and the « Garden of Philosophy », J.-P. Brohez, Summer 1998.

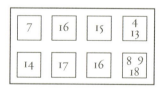
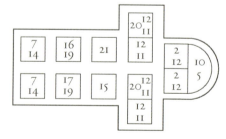

1 Beer and wine
2 Chills
3 Buboes and emollients
4 Plagues and pestilential diseases
5 Fainting
6 Syphilis
7 Gravel
8 Ague
9 Long term fever
10 Headache
11 Tuberculosis
12 Respiratory and pulmonary diseases
13 Sweats and their remedies
14 Gout
15 Cures for vomiting
16 Cures for diarrhoea
17 Purgatives
18 Fleas, bugs and lice
19 Haemorrhoids
20 Osteoarthritis
21 Diseases of the liver

Plan of the « Erasmus Garden » of the « Musée de Saint-Antoine l'Abbaye ». It was made up of three parts : in the basilica grew herbs that where used to heal body organs ; a rectangular area for common ailments and circular basin for plants that grow in water.

The « Garden of Maladies » with A. Vanautgaerden, Henriette and Georges Mees, J.-P. Brohez, Spring 1999.

J.-P. Brohez, Winter 2000.

A tree, A. Jasinski, Spring 2000.

Adage 2
AMICUS, ALTER IPSE
*A friend is
an alter ego*

¶ We gradually came to understand that the structure of the garden described in the *Godly Feast* and the way the nine guests of Eusebius travelled through it was significant in itself. This garden was a « symbolic form », in the sense meant by the philosopher Ernst Cassirer, a machine for conceptualising the world or, rather, a machine for making it habitable and establishing civilised values.
¶ In my opinion, two sayings of Erasmus had to feed the garden spring : *Ubi bene, ibi partia* (« The homeland is where you feel good ») and *Non est muta rerum natura* (« Nature is not dumb. ») This garden had to speak and at the same time explain Erasmus'wanderings. To quote Gilles Clément, the garden of today must be world-wide. ¶ As the garden described in the *Godly Feast* abounded in works of art, I contacted four artists and sent them a draft plan of the garden. I did not want any competition between these artists but preferred a cooperative effort which would enrich the shape the « Philosophical Garden » took. During the year 1998, I met some artists who were already working on themes out of the *Godly Feast* and who would enjoy working together : in a workshop. ¶ Then, in 1999, the landscape architect Benoît Fondu joined our team. At the beginning, he listened a lot before showing us certain developments in garden design we had ignored so far. He also suggested that we should look up at the sky. He opened the space to the space of the clouds.
¶ The garden was not to be a garden of sculptures, nor the putting together of the work of several artists, but a landscaped unity. That's why we worked the soil of our garden together, step by step. We walked, gathered, exchanged ideas, before the picture of this new garden gradually took form. Bob Verschueren was the first to suggest a draft plan, which had a hollow centre, a place of intimacy, which would be the starting point for the different routes. Afterwards, to balance Bob Verschueren's observatory in the centre of the garden, Perejaume suggested a vantage point at the end of the walk in the garden, for looking at the landscape. Thus, we had the centre and the end. After these two first proposals, Catherine Beaugrand suggested marking out the walks in consultation with other artists. Marie-Jo Lafontaine then « balanced » the garden by reflecting the sky in a series of water mirrors.
¶ Benoît Fondu then sketched a new plan of the garden around his leaf-shaped flower beds and as a result of this, the artists' first ideas were somewhat modified. Each artist more or less reformulated his/her first plans so as to find a new overall balance : the garden had become a joint project. ¶ I would like to emphasise here the contribution of the member of our scientific committee because, even though we did not organise many formal meetings, during this whole practical construction stage, we often met its various members informally. They are, in one way or another, responsible for a « part of the garden » : one member contributed by organising a meeting with the landscape architect, the other by drawing my attention to some botanical or landscaping problem, etc. Without these dozens of friendly and brief discussions often held while walking, this garden would still be a paper garden. ¶ In addition to the work in the garden, we thought it was important to reflect on the overall plan of the garden at the same time as we experimented. We therefore invited two photographers, Jasinski and Brohez to join us. We chose André Jasinski for his interest in botany and urban

Benoît Fondu and Perejaume
in July 1999,
A. Vanautgaerden,
Summer 1999.

Max Nowell and Bob
Verschueren in Mei 2000,
J.-P. Brohez,
Spring 2000.

landscape because the museum garden is in the city, subject to problems which are very often more urban than rural. And we invited Jean-Paul Brohez to join us because I realised that a garden is not just a plan and landscape work but first and foremost the daily work of a number of people. It was, therefore, important to keep alive the memory of this joint-venture and of those who put so much effort into it; preferring the harvesting and care of plants to the plant itself. Jean-Paul Brohez loves life and people and we wanted our topiary to express an aspiration towards happiness. These two photographers were joined by four painters : Luc Claus, Bernard Gaube, Félix Hannaert and Aïda Kazarian who immortalised the *genius loci*. Thus, we had begun with the association of a museum curator and a botanist, then we added four artists, an architect, two photographers and four painters : inside, outside, up there, with the stars.

Adage 2048
LIBERI POETÆ ET PICTORES
Free beings, poets and painters

Catherine Beaugrand in August 1999.

Benoît Fondu, Perejaume and Marie-Jo Lafontaine in July 1999.

Bob Verschueren chosing the site of the Observatory in January 2000, A. Vanautgaerden, Winter 2000.

Georges Mees and Perejaume in July 1999, A. Vanautgaerden, Summer 1999.

ARS MECANICA

Ubi machinamentum, quod pone speculum dissimulabatur, intelligebitur.

CATHERINE BEAUGRAND

Adage 2244
AVES QUAERIS
You are looking for birds

THE ARTIST : Catherine Beaugrand lives and works in Paris. Since 1978 has been making works of art which explore the nature of the urban environment and the manner in which the world around us is portrayed. Within the spaces that have been created, and which would be better described as sketches than structures, a dialogue has been set in motion that uses both architectural form and narrative through which Catherine Beaugrand presents the rapid transformation of a space that is open to all. She has recently produced a series of works both on film and in the plastic arts through the medium of theme parks. The most recent one was at the Château de Chambord. She is interested in the different possibilities of linguistic expressions of space in the work « The Godly Feast « where nature shows herself and speaks.

DESCRIPTION : « The first part consists of the production of a site on the theme of friendship. The project is made up of a sort of enclosure of greenery partially encircling a tree. A relationship is established between the two elements, architecture and tree that balance each other as a result of their common origin in nature. ¶ Mapping the garden: The second part of the project comes from the invitation to reflect, in a global manner, on Erasmus' thinking. She has based her work on the central problem in the development of the project; that is to create routes or moments in the form of short lines, which interact with the other projects. These lines are formed by *loci - locus* in the sense of « container » These containers produce a sort of genius loci by their position. The containers are made of identical material and are of identical shape. Their size, their position and their use are always different. However, their character and nature impose certain rules on these – they can be placed in the soil, they can stand, lie or be lifted up. Between simplicity of form and the idea of their relationships; between the linearity of the sequential process and the different viewpoints made possible by interrelationships with other projects; between perceptions that follow each other as you walk and moments of still contemplation; between journeying and vanishing point, these *loci* are possible pathways of transformation. »
(Catherine Beaugrand)
SIZE : 2,60 m (height)
MATERIAL : 11 Fagus sylvatica (Beeches)
CREATION : Plantation service of Anderlecht.

You could consider the « Godly Feast » as a picture that you travel across. House and gardens together make a place where the perspective changes as you advance, in order to communicate new and unexpected meanings. Even the way in which the windows open produces different viewpoints and gives a different atmosphere, depending on the season. Movements connect the events that are scattered across the space. You could say that it is just these discontinuities, moments, settings that cause the space to exist. What you experience during your journey in the enclosed garden is also to be found on the larger scale of journeys through Europe.
(Catherine Beaugrand)

EXHIBITIONS (SELECTION) : ¶ 1978 : Sol Gallery Lyons. ¶ 1983 : Mercato del Sale Gallery, Milan. ¶ 1986 : « Concert privé », Hôtel Particulier, Lyons. ¶ 1987 : Westersingle Gallery, Rotterdam. ¶ 1989 : « Tantôt Roi Tantôt Reine », CNAP, Paris / Museum of Contemporary Art, Lyons. ¶ 1990 : « Ava Pandora », Museum of Contemporary Art, Lyons / Sylvana Lorenz Gallery, Paris. ¶ 1994 : « Le Masque de la Mort Rouge », Museum of Art and History, Ashiya / Museum of Kitakanto, Maebashi. ¶ 1995 : « Pacifique comme un homme courageux », Scène Nationale, Evreux. ¶ 1996 : Centre d'Art Contemporain, Vassivière / Jacqueline Moussion Gallery, Paris. ¶ 1998 : « Panorama », Centre d'Art, Rueil / UME-SE, Umea, Sweden. ¶ 1999 : Historical Monuments, Nadiff, Tokyo. ¶ 2000 : « Projet Holbein », Art Front Gallery, Tokyo / Le Quartier, Quimper.
JOINT EXHIBITIONS (SELECTION) : ¶ 1980 : « Made in France », ELAC, Lyons. ¶ 1982 : « Faire Semblant », Museum of Painting, Grenoble. ¶ 1983 : « Ces Dames aux Chapeaux Verts », Maison des Expositions, Genas. ¶ 1984 : « Cent Oeuvres, Soixante-quinze Artistes », CNAP, Paris / « Collections », Museum of Contemporary Art, Lyons. ¶ 1985 : « Soyons Sérieux », ELAC, Lyons. ¶ 1986 : « Prospect 86 », Kunstverein, Frankfurt. ¶ 1987 : « Mnemosyne oder das Theater der Erinnerung », Worms. ¶ 1989 : « Tantôt Roi Tantôt Reine », Museum of Contemporary Art, Lyons / « R. Hains, A. Cadere, C.Beaugrand », PS 1 Museum, New York / Trigon 89, « Aktuelle », Neue Galerie, Graz. ¶ 1990 : « Zeitgenossische Kunst im stadtischen Raum », Frankfurt. ¶ 1991 : « 14 individualités françaises », Art Gallery of

Ontario, Toronto / « Stillstand : Switches », Shedalle, Zurich / « L'Amour de l'Art », Biennale d'Art Contemporain, Lyons. ¶ 1992 : « Les Iconodules », Biennale des Musées de Normandie, Evreux. ¶ 1994 : « RN 86, l'Art, la Ville, la Route », Institut pour l'Art et la Ville, Givors / Sylvana Lorenz Gallery, Paris. ¶ 1995 : Jacqueline Moussion Gallery, Paris / Biennale d'Art Contemporain, Lyons. ¶ 1996 : « Tapisseries récentes », Commandes publiques, Aubusson Museum. ¶ 1997 : « Documenta X », Kassel / « V.O. », IVe Biennale de Lyons. ¶ 1998 : « P.O. BOX », Mamco, Geneva / « In Situ », Biennale d'Art Public, Enghien / « Mediterranea », Le Botanique, Brussels. ¶ 1999 : « Duchampiana », MAMCO, Geneva / « Sonne, Mond und Sterne », Kokerei Zollverein, Essen / « Scattered affinities », Fundacion Arte y Tecnologia, Madrid / « Collection Gilbert Monin », Maison de l'Image et du Son, Villeurbanne / « Xe Anniversaire », Centre d'Art Contemporain, Vassivière / « Dessine-moi une École », Académie des Arts Visuels, Leipzig / Collections, Museum of Contemporary Art, Yokohama / « Salon d'actualités », Institut Français d'Architecture, Paris. ¶ 2000, Singen / « Le rêve du ciel » in *Changement de temps*, Château de Chambord.
BIBLIOGRAPHY (1 BOOK): A monography will be edited in September 2000 by the Contemporary Art Center, Le Quartier, Quimper.

MARIE-JO LAFONTAINE

THE ARTIST : Marie-Jo Lafontaine lives and works in Brussels. Since the end of the 1970's she has developed a style which is influenced by the passions of violence and desire, but also by the fragility of the world. Since the middle of the 1990's she has increasingly filmed and photographed the four elements: she has made pictures with water, fire and clouds. The work that she has created at the Erasmus Museum is related to the impermanence and fragility of the world: it is a reflection.
DESCRIPTION : 7 almond-shaped basins of different sizes full of water. They are connected together by a system of communicating vessels. The water is level with the grass. Slightly below the water level, an adage of Erasmus (different in each basin) can be read in metal letters. The ground of each basin is covered with marble gravel which darkens the surface of the water, acting as a mirror.
ADAGES : ¶ 1012 : *Difficilia quæ pulchra* (« Beautiful things are difficult ») ¶ 1193 : *Ubi bene ibi patria* [*Quavis terra patria*] (« Your homeland is where you feel good ») ¶ 201 : *Aut regem, aut fatuum nasci oportere* (« You must born either as a king or a fool ») ¶ 224 : *Ubi amici, ibi opes* « Your wealth is where your friends are » ¶ Epistola 1314 : *Civis mundi sum, communis omnium vel peregrinus magis* (« I am a citizen of the world, my homeland is everywhere, or rather, I am a foreigner to everyone ») ¶ 3144 : *Sidera addere cælo* (« Add stars to the sky ») ¶ 1001 : *Festina lente* (« More haste, less speed »).
SIZE : 2 basins of 7,40 x 1,65 m ; 1 of 7,10 x 1,60 m ; 1 of 5,80 x 1,50 m ; 2 of 5,20 x 1,40 m and 1 of 4,70 x 1,25 m.
MATERIAL : galvanised steel (basins), marble (at the bottom of the basins), brass (letters), water.
CREATION : Garsy (basins), Vamor (cutting of letters), Verheyden (hydraulic system).

PERSONAL EXHIBITIONS (SELECTION) : ¶ 1976 : Walter Thompson Gallery, Brussels ¶ 1979 : Palais des Beaux-Arts, Brussels (cat.) / I.C.C., Antwerp. ¶ 1981 : National Museum of Modern Art, Centre Georges Pompidou, Paris ¶ 1982 : CAPC, Bordeaux. ¶ 1983 : Maison de la Culture, La Rochelle / Haags Gemeentemuseum, The Hague. ¶ 1984 : National Museum of Modern Art, Centre Georges Pompidou, Paris / Powerhouse Gallery, Montréal / Octobre des Arts, E.L.A.C., Lyons. ¶ 1985 : Maison de la Culture, La Rochelle / Cirque Divers, Liège / Maison de la Culture, Le Havre / Carpenter Center, Harvard University, Boston / Tate Gallery, London (cat.) / Museum of Modern Art, Villeneuve d'Ascq (cat.). ¶ 1986 : Cantini Museum, Marseille (cat.) / Pétrarque Room, Montpellier / Sprengel Museum, Hannover. ¶ 1987 : Brou Museum, Bourg-en-Bresse (cat.) / Gemeentemuseum, Arnhem / de Gryse Gallery, Tielt / Centre d'Art contemporain, Orléans / Koninkelijk Muziekconservatorium, Ghent / Roger Pailhas Gallery, Marseilles. ¶ 1988 : Los Angeles County Museum of Art, Los Angeles (cat.) / Museum für Gegenwartskunst, Basle (cat.) / Walter Storms Gallery, Munich / Wanda Reiff Gallery, Maastricht (cat.) / Forum, Walter Storms Gallery, Hamburg. ¶ 1989 : Jack Shainmann Gallery, New York / Weisses Haus,

Adage 1293
E SCILLA
NON NASCITUR ROSA
A rose is not born from a shellfish

Territory is a space, a space that you occupy. The primal space is that between your two arms: your body. Your body is your first space. Afterwards, you have to conquer the rest. I think that this is something important. For me, in any case, it was important to conquer it and see how this process of conquest takes place.
(Marie-Jo Lafontaine)

Hamburg (cat.) / Michael Horbach Gallery, Cologne / Fruitmarket Gallery, Edinburgh (cat.) / Whitechapel Art Gallery, London (cat.) / Musée Communal, Luxembourg. ¶ 1990 : Arco, Walter Storms Gallery, Madrid / Städtisches Museum Abteiberg, Mönchengladbach (cat.) / Salzburger Kunstverein, Salzburg (cat.) / Städtisches Museum Schloss Hardenberg, Velbert (cat.) / Städtische Gallery, Göppingen (cat.) / Musée des Beaux Arts, Tourcoing / Montaigne Gallery, Paris (cat.) ¶ 1991 : Wewerka- Weiss Gallery, Berlin / Ric Urmel Gallery, Ghent / Bergkerk Kunst, Deventer (cat.) / Walter Storms Gallery, Munich. ¶ 1992 : Beaumont Gallery, Luxembourg / Archief, The Hague / Montaigne gallery, Paris / Vereins und Westbank, Hamburg / Museum für Kunst, Lübeck / Nordjyllands Kunstmuseum, Aalborg (cat.) / Goethe Institute, Brussels / Museum of Art, Tel Aviv (cat.). ¶ 1993 : Bugdahn und Kaimer gallery, Düsseldorf / Galerij Deweer, Ottegem (cat.) ¶ 1994 : Smith College Museum, Massachussets (cat.) / Lisboa 94, Lisbon (cat.) / Galeria Comicos, Lisbon / University Art Museum, Long Beach, California (cat.) / Wanâs, Knislinge / Gasometer, Oberhausen (cat.) / Bugdahn und Kaimer Gallery, Düsseldorf / Walter Storms Gallery, Cologne . ¶ 1995 : Thaddaeus Ropac Gallery, Paris / de Gryse Gallery, Tielt, Belgique / Rigassi Gallery, Bern (cat.) / Thaddaeus Ropac Gallery, Salzburg / Festspielhaus « Die Muse », Salzburg (cat.) ¶ 1996 : Thaddaeus Roppac Gallery, Salzburg / Bugdahn und Kaimer Gallery, Düsseldorf / Wanda Reiff Gallery, Maastricht. ¶ 1997 : Bugdahn und Kaimer Gallery, Düsseldorf ¶ 1998 : Site / Gallery, Sheffield / de Gryse Gallery, Tielt / BBL Gallery, Kortrijk (cat.) / Bundesakademie, Wölfenbüttel / Galleria Civica d'Arte Moderna, Palermo / The Orchard Gallery, Derry / Erban, Nantes. ¶ 1999 : Beaumont Gallery, Luxembourg / Mathildehöhe Institute, Darmstad / Galerie nationale du Jeu de Paume, Paris (CD-ROM) / Odepark, Venray / Museum voor Hedendaagse Kunst, Ghent.
JOINT EXHIBITIONS (SELECTION) : ¶ 1978 : « Prix de la Jeune Peinture Belge », Palais des Beaux-Arts, Brussels. 1985 : A.R.C.A., Marseilles. ¶ 1986 : « Chambres d'Amis », Ghent. ¶ 1987 : « Documenta 8 », Kassel (cat.). ¶ 1988 : « Mnemosyne oder das Theater der Erinnerung », Schloss Herrnsheim, Worms (cat.). ¶ 1990 : « Threshold », National Museum of Contemporary Art, Oslo (cat.). ¶ 1992 : « Moving Image », Fundacio Joan Miro, Barcelona, (cat.) / « Tradition der Moderne » I.G. Metal Gewerkschaft, Frankfurt ; Stuttgart ; Berlin / « Word and Image », Museum van Hedendaagse Kunst, Antwerp (cat.). ¶ 1993 : « Feuer, Wasser, Licht, Erde », Deichtorhallen, Hamburg (cat.) / Museum of Modern Art, Omiya (cat.) / « Retrospectives installations vidéos », Museum van Hedendaagse Kunst, Antwerp (cat.). ¶ 1995 : ARS 95, Museum of Contemporary Art, Helsinki (cat.) / « Jeder Engel ist schrecklich », Gasometer, Oberhausen (cat.). ¶ 1998 : « Pandemonium », Fruitmarket Gallery, Edinburgh. ¶ 1999 : « Démarches », Muzeumzaal, Louvain.
BIBLIOGRAPHY (1 BOOK) : *Marie-Jo Lafontaine,* Ostfildern-Ruit, Hatje Cantz Publishers, 1999 [DU/ENG]
CD-ROM : *Marie-Jo Lafontaine. Installations Vidéos 1979-1999,* Paris, Réunion des Musées Nationaux et Galerie nationale du Jeu de Paume, 1999 [FR/ENG]

PEREJAUME

Adage 3660
IN CRASTINUM SERIA
Serious matters are for tomorrow

THE ARTIST : Perejaume works and lives in Catalonia at San Pol de Mar. Since the 1970's he has developed a style which explores the idea of landscape and reflects on its portrayal with the help of paintings, sculptures and poems. Perjaume sees the world as an immense exhibition gallery in which he can place his topographical works, which show how this world was constructed. The work that he has made for the « Philosophical Garden », a « folly » in the old-fashioned sense, is a vantage point from which to observe the landscape. It is similar to the structures that were used by walkers in parks and landscapes in the 18th century, in order to appreciate better the artistic character of nature.
DESCRIPTION : A gazebo composed of 83 stained-glass panels and including an opening allowing walkers to go into the structure and observe landscape of the garden.
SIZE : 3,60 x 2,40 x 1,80 m.
MATERIAL : Steel covered with copper (structure), 11.500 glass lenses, lead.
CREATION : Marta Depazurueña and Montserrat Sarmientojuan from the Centro del Vidre de Barcelona (stained glass), Garsy S.A. (structure).

BOOKS WRITTEN BY PEREJAUME : ¶ 1989 : *Ludwig-Jujol. Què és el collage, sinó acostar soledats ? Lluís II de Baviera, Josep Maria Jujol,* Barcelona, La Magrana. ¶ 1989 : *Fragmente der Monarchie.* with texts by Andrea Tschechow, Erik Mosel and Joan Tarrida, Munich, Mosel und Tschechow. ¶ 1992 : *Oli damunt paper,* Barcelona, Empúries. ¶ 1993 : *La Pintura i la Boca,* Barcelona, La Magrana (Cotlliure ; 19). ¶ 1995 : *El Paisatge és rodó,* Vic, H., Eumo, Associació per a les Arts Contemporànies / *Nocturn : Miquel Campeny, Nicolau Raurich, Joaquim Pou, Benet Martorell,* with Jordi Pomés, Sant Pol de Mar, Museu de Pintura. ¶ 1997 : *El Pirineu de Baix. Mont-Roig, Miró, Mallorca,* with texts by Vicenç Altaió, William Jeffett and Michael Pennie, Barcelona, Polígrafa. ¶ 1998 : *Diürn : Ignasi Mas, Avi Vila,* with texts by Juan José Lahuerta, Sant Pol de Mar, Museu de Pintura / *Oïsme,* prologue by Joseph Palau et Fabre, Barcelona, Proa. ¶ 1999 : *Oleoducte,* Barcelona, Polígrafa.
PERSONAL EXHIBITIONS (SELECTION) : ¶ 1978 : « Pintures », Ciento Gallery, Barcelona ¶ 1979 : Sa Pleta Freda Gallery, Majorca ¶ 1980 : « Olis i objectes », Joan Prats Gallery, Barcelona ¶ 1983 : « Exposició al bosc de can Montells », Cardedeu / Joan Prats Gallery, Barcelona ¶ 1984 : Mataró, Can Xammar ¶ 1985 : « Figueres », Massanet Gallery / « Postaler », Fundació Caixa de Pensions, Sala Montcada, Barcelona ¶ 1986 : « Marcs », Sabadell, Museu d'Art, Espai 83 / « Pintures, escultures, instal-lacions, videos », Joan Prats Galleria, Barcelona ¶ 1987 : Montenegro Gallery, Madrid / Centre Régional d'Art Contemporain Midi-Pyrénées, Toulouse ¶ 1988 : « A 2000 metres de pintura sobre el nivell del mar », Tinglado 2, Tarragona / « Pintura y representación », Montenegro Gallery, Madrid ¶ 1989 : « L'ombra », Col-legi Oficial d'Aparelladors i Arquitectes Tècnics de Barcelona, Anar i Tornar, Barcelona / « Marea-Tide », Joan Prats Gallery-Milford Gallery, New York / « Viatge », Fundació Joan Miró, Barcelona ¶ 1990 : « Escala », Städtische Gallery im Lenbachhaus, Munich / « Coll de Pal-Cim del Costabona », Joan Prats Gallery, Barcelona ¶ 1991 : « Broadway Window Installation », The New Museum of Contemporary Art, New York / « Dos geografías », Windsor Kulturgintza, Bilbao / « Dues Geografies », Galeria Graça Fonseca, Lisbon / « El grado de la Verdad de las representaciones », Soledad Lorenzo Gallery, Madrid / « Künstler. Kritisches Lexikon der Gegenwartskunst », Weltkunst und Bruckmann, Munich / « Pintura per a exteriors », Fundació Joan Miró, Espai 13, Barcelona ¶ 1992 : Expo 92, Sevilla / « Pinacoteques », Joan Prats Gallery,-Artgràfics, Barcelona ¶ 1993 : « Landscapes and long distances », Arnolfini Gallery, Anderson O'Day Gallery, London / « Perejaume : Mont-Roig », Mont-Roig, Església Vella ¶ 1994 : Ghent, Museum van Hedendaagse Kunst / « Pintures », Barcelona, Joan Prats gallery / « Terra de suro », Céret, Musée d'art moderne de Céret ¶ 1995 : « Perejaume : diciembre, enero, Febrero, marzo », Burgos, Caja de Burgos ¶ 1997 : « Perejaume : Girona, Sant Pol, Pineda i la Vall d'Oo », Girona, Ajuntament de Girona / Ajuntament de Sant Pol de Mar / Ajuntament de Pineda i la Vall d'Oo / « Perejaume : Tres dibuixos », Saint-Jacques de Compostelle, Centro Galego de Arte Contemporánea.
JOINT EXHIBITIONS (SELECTION) : ¶ 1979 : « La seconda vanguardia catalana »,Viareggio, Palazzo Paolina. ¶ 1983 : « Casino », Sabadell, Èczema / Perpignian, Symptômes / Montpellier, MEDaMothi. ¶ 1984 : « Nits », Barcelona, Fundació Caixa de Pensions. ¶ 1987 : « Naturalezas espanolas 1940-1987 », Madrid, Centro de Arte Reina Sofía. ¶ 1988 : « Acta 88 », Madrid, Palacio de Velázquez / « Arts escrits : Joan Brossa, Perejaume, Benet Rossel, Antonio Saura, Antoni Tàpies », Lleida, Institut d'Estudis Ilerdencs. ¶ 1989 : « Die Spanische Kunst in der Sammlung der Fundació 'la Caixa de Pensions' » / « Les grâces de la nature. Sixièmes ateliers internationaux des Pays de la Loire », Garenne Lemot, Le parc de la Garenne Lemot / « Mediterraneo per l'arte contemporanea », Bari, Regione Puglia Assessorato alla cultura / « What is contemporary art ? », Malmö, Rooseum Center for Contemporary Art ¶ 1990 : « 6 Katalanische Künstler », Ludwigsburg, Kunstverein Ludwigsburg / « Art espagnol des années 80 dans les collections de la Fundació Caixa de Pensions », Labege, Centre Régional d'Art Contemporain Midi-Pyrénées / « La creación artística como cuestionamiento », Valence, IVAM / « Imágenes líricas. New Spanish visions », Long Beach, University Art Museum / California State University / « La Biennale di Venezia », Venise, Biennale de Venise / « Sculpture contemporaine espagnole », Paris, Ministère de la Culture, de la Communication, des Grands travaux et du Bicentenaire / Barcelona, Santa Mònica Art Centre. ¶ 1991 : « Das Goldene Zeitalter », Stuttgart, Wüttembergischer Kunstverein / « Formes de la dissensió », Barcelona, Fundació Joan Miró.

True nature, that is to say, virgin space, only exists within us. You can turn the terms on their heads and say, for example, that the whole planet is a garden, successful or otherwise; or there again, that working in a garden or in a museum gallery is a [burden] and similarly, working on a garden is not working on nature herself, but on a painting made of nature. Contemporary art is shot through with a sort of general confusion – nature / garden, painting / reality, literature / existence, etc., but we must continue to work at the frontiers. (Perejaume)

Espai 13 / « Kunst, Europa : 63 deutsche Kunstvereine zeigen Kunst aus 20 Ländern », Mayence, Herman Schmidt / « L'Exposition de l'École du Magasin », Grenoble, Centre national d'art contemporain de Grenoble. ¶ 1992 : « Dels trobadors a la poesia actual », Barcelona, Laertes / « Ceci n'est pas une sculpture : I und II, Munich, Musel und Tschechow / « Barcelona abroad : Pep Agut, Jordi Colomer, Ramon Parramon, Perejaume », Ipswich, European Visual Arts / « Espagne, 23 artistes pour l'an 2000 : peintures et sculptures », Paris, Artcurial / « Na Miró. Kunstwerken van de hedendaagse Catalaanse kunst », Amsterdam / « The Boundary rider 9th Biennale of Sydney. ¶ 1993 : « Différentes natures : visions de l'art contemporain », Torí, Lindau / La Défense, Établissement public pour l'aménagement de la Défense / « Arte espanol contemporáneo », Marugame, Marugame Museum, Hirai. / 1994 : « Züge Züge - die Eisenbahn in der Zeitgenössichen Kunst », Esslingen, Galerie der Stadt / Goppingen, Märklin Museum. ¶ 1995 : « Fundación Coca Cola Espana. / « Thinking of you a selection of contemporary Spanish art », Götteborg, Konsthallen. ¶ 1997 : « La construcción de la naturaleza », Valence, Generalitat Valenciana. ¶ 1999 : « Viva Wagner ! », Bayreuth, Richard Wagner Museum.
BIBLIOGRAPHY (1 BOOK) : *Perejaume. Dis–exhibit*, Barcelona, MACBA, 1999.

BOB VERSCHUEREN

Adage 2024
BONA TERRAE
The good things of the earth

THE ARTIST : Bob Verschueren lives and works in Wauthier-Braine (B). He gave up painting in 1978 and since then has based his work on nature (wind, light, vegetation, sound etc.) using perishable materials. The Observatory in the 'Philosophical Garden' is the first permanent work that he has produced. In fact, it's a question of timeframe, as the stump of the beech tree will also finally disappear under moss and the action of water. Bob Verschueren works with the energy of nature, which, to a greater or lesser degree, always has the last word in the final form of his works.
DESCRIPTION : An observatory, in the earth, surrounded by a wall. A spiral-shaped ramp allows walkers to go down. In the centre, a charred tree stump is used as a fountain covered by moss and filamentous seaweed.
SIZE : 5.11 m (diameter), 1 m (depth).
MATERIAL : 13 tons of tuff (« Moon rock »), the stump of an ancient beech from the estate of the Seneffe Castle, a hydraulic system, moss and filamentous seaweed.
CREATION : The dry stone wall was built by two masons, a Scotsman (Max Nowell) and an Englishman (Andrew Loudon). The stump was « prepared » by the Belgian tree-trimmer Christian Cauwe.

My work speaks about the relationship between life and death, and in so doing, rehabilitates death to a certain extent, but without morbidity. It speaks also of the eternal nature of a work of art, of the essence of permanence, and, of course, of our own temporality.
(Bob Verschueren)

EXHIBITIONS WITH CREATION OF WORKS OF ART 'IN SITU' (SELECTION) : ¶ 1983 : Aarschot (B), Speelhoven, *Speelhoven '83* (cat.) ¶ 1985 : Brussels (B), Atelier 340, *De l'Animal et du Végétal dans l'art belge contemporain* (cat.) / Warsaw (PL), Galeria ZAR, *Powierzchnia rzezbiarska [Sculptural area]* (cat.) ¶ 1986 : Krakow(PL), Palais des Beaux-Arts, *Powierzchnia rzezbiarska [Sculptural area]* (cat.) / Brussels (B), Plus-Kern Gallery, *Bob Verschueren. « Paperworks »* (cat.) / Ghent (B), Fabriek van Entetarde Kunst, *Antichambre* (cat.) / Ghent (B), At Work, Rob Bruyninckx, Marc Lambrechts, Bob Verschueren (*Initiatief '86*) (cat.) / Assenede (B), *A(rt)ssenede '86* (cat.) / Brussels (B), Atelier 340, *Matières non assemblées dans l'art belge contemporain* (cat.) / Harelbeke (B), Stedelijke Academie, *Beelden in en rond het Ontmoetingscentrum* (cat.) ¶ 1987 : Liege (B), Musée d'art moderne, *Surface sculpturale* (cat.) / Antwerp (B), Zuiderpershuis, *Associations momentanées '87* (cat.) / Brussels (B), Atelier 340, *Piet Stockmans - Bob Verschueren* (cat.) / Le Havre (F), Festival d'été de Normandie, *Quand on sème. /* Mariemont (B), Drève de Mariemont, *Articulture 2* (cat.) / Louvain (B), different places, *Alchemie*. ¶ 1988 : Aachen (D), Neue Galerie - Sammlung Ludwig, *Tierisches und Pflanzliches in der Zeitgenössichen Belgischen Kunst* (cat.) / Antwerp (B), Galerie Het Roze Huis / Apeldoorn (NL), Van Reekum Museum, *Het dierlijke en plaantardige in de hedendaagse Belgische kunst* (cat.) ¶ 1989 : Montreal (CDN), Galerie Trois-Points, *Bob Verschueren - installations végétales & Bernard Gaube - peintures récentes* / Liege (B), different places, *Fenêtres en vue* (cat.) / Binche (B), different places, *Ramp'Art* (cat.) / Arlon (B), different places, *Pour l'art public. Avec Christian Claus,* EUX TROIS, *Stéphan Gilles, Chantal Talbot,* TOUT / Montreal (CDN), Maison de la Culture du Plateau Mont-Royal. / Montreal (CDN), Maison de la Culture Mercier. ¶ 1990 : Bruges (B), Galerij 't Leerhuys, *Bob Verschueren – Jean-Georges Massart* / Bottrop (D), Josef Albers Museum Quadrat / Lommel

(B), *Lommel 1990 – Kunstprojekt 1* (cat.) ¶ 1991 : Brussels (B), Chapelle des Brigittines. / Hamois (B), Espace Partenaires - Mises en oeuvres. *De l'esquisse au site* (cat.) / Brussels (B), BBL (Cours Saint-Michel) (cat.). ¶ Ghent,-Mariakerke (B), Beukenhof, *A Taste of Earth - I* (cat.) ¶ 1992 : Eke (B), Galerij Labo Art, *Landschap 92* / Brussels (B), Atelier 340, *Nils-Udo - Bob Verschueren. Avec arbres et feuilles* (cat.) / Brussels (B), Philip Morris Belgium. / Chicoutimi (CDN), *Espace virtuel, Bob Verschueren.* / Rimouski (CDN), Regional Museum. ¶ 1993 : Montreal (CDN), *Dazibao, Ariane Thézé et Bob Verschueren* (cat.) / Antwerp (B), Cultureel Centrum Berchem, *Paradise Lost* (cat.) / Brussels (B), Espace photographique Contretype, *Ariane Thézé et Bob Verschueren.* / Aachen (D), garden of the Ludwig Forum für internationale Kunst (cat.) / Poznan (PL), Arsenal, Galeria Miejska, Nils-Udo - Bob Verschueren. / Orval (B), Abbaye Notre-Dame. / Bad Dürkheim (D), Burgkirche, *Bob Verschueren. Natur Zeit Geometrie.* / Ludwigshafen am Rhein (D), Wilhelm-Hack-Museum, *Bob Verschueren. Natur Zeit Geometrie.* / « Le Four à verre » (B), chez M. et Mme Sulmon-Gillieaux. / Matane (CDN), Matane Art Gallery. / Hasselt (B), Provinciaal Museum. ¶ 1994 : Budapest (H), Múcsarnok (Kiállítási Csarnok), *Nils-Udo - Bob Verschueren. Fával és levelekkel* [with trees and leafs]. / Aschaffenburg (D), Im Kornhäuschen, Webergasse. / Jaulny (F), lavoir public, dans le cadre du projet *Architecture & Nature* (cat.). Org. : FRAC Lorraine / Luxembourg (L), Cercle municipal. / Bochum (D), Kunstverein (« Haus Kemnade »), *Kunst, natürlich,* avec Daniel Bräg, Rolf Julius, Mathis Neidhart, Mario Reis, Timm Ulrich (cat.) ¶ 1995 : Brussels (B), Atelier 340, *L'Atelier 340 a 15 ans* / Paris (F), Galerie Moussion. / Amsterdam (NL), Stichting Open Space. ¶ 1996 : Le Blanc-Mesnil (F), Forum culturel (and different places in Seine-Saint-Denis), *Art grandeur nature 1996* (cat.) / Amsterdam (NL), *Rai, KunstRai 96* (avec la Stichting Open Space) (cat.) / Saint-Vaast-La-Hougue (F), Musée maritime de l'Île Tatihou, *Anne Delfieu, Roland Cognet, Bob Verschueren* (cat.) / Oronsko (PL), Centrum Rzezby Polskiej. ¶ 1997 : Louvain (B), différents lieux, *Nature Morte??* (cat.) / Brussels (B), Atelier 340, Bob Verschueren, *Exposition monographique* (cat.) / Burgh-Haamstede (NL), De Bewaarschool, *Een ongekende schittering - Bob Verschueren.* (cat.) / Calais (F), Ancienne Poste Gallery. ¶ 1998 : Arles (F), Cloître Saint Trophime et Musée Réattu (cat.) / Erfurt (D), Hauptbahnhof, *Exposition monographique.* / Louvain-la-Neuve (B), Musée de Louvain-la-Neuve, *L'Art au toucher.* / Brussels (B), Atelier 340, *Amorce de la collection.* / Verviers (B), *Arte Coppo.* / Tourinnes la Grosse (B), different places, *Christian Rolet invite...* / Liège (B), Museum of Modern Art and Contemporary Art, *L'arbre qui cache la forêt* (cat.) ¶ 1999 : Geneva (CH), Guy Bärtschi Gallery. / Poznan, Galeria R. / Île de la Réunion, Lieu Art Contemporain. / Liège (B), Saint-Georges Room, *Quand soufflent les vents du Sud – aujourd'hui artistes en Wallonie.* ¶ 2000 : Brussels (B), Chapelle de Boendael. / Namur, Maison de la culture. / Borgo Valsugana (I), Arte Sella.

OTHERS EXHIBITIONS (SELECTION) : ¶ 1982 : Antwerp (B), Vécu Gallery, *Windpaintings.* ¶ 1983 : Brussels (B), Château Malou, *Square – Événement autour d'une oeuvre biodégradable* (cat.) / Brussels (B), Théâtre de Banlieue. ¶ 1988 : Brussels (B), ISELP, *Pages d'artistes hors mesure. Cinquante fois Plus Moins Zéro* (cat.) / Montreal (CDN), Transpose Gallery, *II*e *festival international de photographie actuelle* (cat.) / La Vénerie. ¶ 1989 : Kyoto (JAP), International Art Centre, International Impact Art Festival 89 (cat.) ¶ 1992 : Brussels (B), Fondation européenne de la sculpture, Parc Tournay-Solvay, *Des sculpteurs et des arbres* (cat.) With Jephan de Villiers, Philippe Le Docte, Anne Nuthals, André Willequet. ¶ 1993 : Verviers (B), Musée des Beaux-Arts, *Aspects actuels de la mouvance construite internationale. Section I : Mesures art international et ses amis* (cat.) / Rabat (MA), Bab-El-Rouah Gallery, *Quinzaine Maroc-Wallonie.* ¶ 1994 : Antwerp (B), ICC, *Aspecten van de hedendaagse constructieve beweging* (cat.) / Jamoigne (B), Grange du Faing, « *Semois - Semoy - Itinéraire* ». *Projet pour une réflexion sur le paysage contemporain* [non réalisé]. ¶ 1995 : Amsterdam , Stichting Open Space, *Bob Verschueren. Fototentoonstelling* (cat.) / Remscheid (D), ART & RAT Gallery, *Durchröntgen. Lichtbilder zum Jubiläum eines Forschers und Entdeckers* (cat.) Travelling exhibition : (25/2-24/3/96) Recklinghausen (D), Kunstverein. ¶ 1998 : Brussels (B), Le Botanique, *Dérives botaniques* (cat.) ¶ 1999 : Brussels (B), ISELP, *Libertés, libertés chéries ou l'Art comme résistance à l'Art* (cat.)

SCENOGRAPHIES : ¶ 1983 : *Incubation, du groupe Ourva.* Created in the Théâtre de Banlieue, Brussels (B). ¶ 1993 : *Ophélia's,* by Alain Populaire et Elisabeth Maesen. Created in the Chapelle des Brigittines, Brussels (B). ¶ 1999 : *Anima fragila,* by the Irene K. Company Created in the Ludwig Forum für internationale Kunst, Aachen (D).

BIBLIOGRAPHY (1 BOOK) : *Bob Verschueren*, Brussels, Atelier 340, 1997 [FR/DU/ENG/GE]

Jean-Paul Brohez

Adage 3153
Audi chelidonem
Listen to the swallow

THE ARTIST : Live and works at Ellemelle (B), a village between Namur and Huy. *Homo viator,* he travels the world like Erasmus: in order to see.
PUBLICATIONS (SELECTION) : ¶ 1985 : *Bruissage,* Brussels, Éd. du Stratège. ¶ 1986 : *Faits d'hiver,* Liege, SDC. ¶ 1986 : *Cartographie,* Liege, SDC. ¶ 1989 : *Vues de Liège,* Liege, Homme et ville. ¶ 1994 : *Temps morts,* Crisnée, Éd. Yellow Now. / *De l'utopie au réel,* Liège, Chiroux cultural centre / Homme et ville. ¶ 1994 : *B 8,* collectif, Brussels, La Lettre volée et Contretype. ¶ 1999 : *Couleur locale,* Crisnée, Éd. Yellow Now, programmation on CD-ROM, original music by Garett List. ¶ 2000 : *N'oublie pas que les oiseaux chantent,* Ellemelle, Semence de curieux.

André Jasinski

Adage 3299
Statua taciturnior
More silent than a statue

THE PHOTOGRAPHER : André Jasinski lives and works in Brussels. He often photographs townscapes, which show ruins and neglect. In these deserted places he saves both nature and industrial archaeology for posterity. He photographed the garden both by day and night.

EXHIBITIONS (SELECTION) : ¶ 1999 : Centre de diffusion Clark, Montreal (CND). / Montreal (CND), Trois Points Gallery. / Brussels (B), Le Salon d'Art Gallery. / Périscope Gallery, Liege (B). ¶ 1998 : Coimbra (P), XVIII° *Encontros de Fotografia.* ¶ 1997 :   Quebec (CND),Centre Vu. / Antwerp (B), Museum voor Fotografie. ¶ 1994 : Charleroi (B), Palais des Beaux-Arts, *Les Concessions du Hasard.* ¶ 1992 : Barcelona (E), Fondation Joan Miro, Primavera Fotografica de Barcelona, *Holzwege.* ¶ 1991 : Brussels (B), Espace Photographique Contretype, *Holzwege.* / Coimbra (P), XI° Encontros de Fotografia, Circolo de Artes Plasticas. / Reims (F), Intérieur Actuel Gallery, *Mai de la photo.* ¶ 1989 : Charleroi (B), Musée de la Photographie, *Les Concessions du Hasard.* ¶ 1988 : Brussels (B), Le Salon d'Art Gallery, *Pièges à lumières.*
JOINT EXHIBITIONS (SELECTION) : ¶ 2000 : Brussels (B), Anciennes Glacières de Saint-Gilles, *Bruxelles à l'infini.* / Brussels (B), Le Botanique, *Bruxelles (une ville) en photographie.* ¶ 1999 : Brussels (B), Espace Photographique Contretype, *Bruxelles exposant 8.* ¶ 1998 : Le Mans (F), Paul Courboulay Exhibitions Room, XVII° *Festival de l'image.* ¶ 1997 : Liege (B), Museum of Modern Art and Contemporary Art, *Sites et cités.* ¶ 1996 : Recklinghausen (D), Kutscherhaus, *Durch Röntgen.* ¶ 1995 : Geneva (CH), Centre Saint-Gervais, *La ville et son cliché.* / Brussels (B), Espace Photographique Contretype, *La ville et son cliché.* / Grand-Hornu Site (B), *L'autre voie.* / Remscheid (D), Art & Rat Gallery, *Durch Röntgen.* / Liege (B), Académie Royale des Beaux-Arts, *Train & création.* ¶ 1994 : Paris (F), Colbert Gallery, Mois de la photo à Paris, *La matière, l'ombre, la fiction.* / Paris (F), Centre Wallonie-Bruxelles, Mois de la photo à Paris, *Ville en éclats.* / Barcelona (E), Fondation Joan Miro, *Corpus delicti.* / Houston (U.S.A), Museum of Fine Arts, *Tradition and the Unpredictable.* ¶ 1993 : Charleroi (B), Musée de la Photographie, *Le noir est blanc.* / Paris (F), Espace Gran Dia, *Zinc, épreuves d'artistes.* / Zonnebeke (B), Kunstencentrum De Poort, *Lichtekooi.* / Évry (F), Théâtre de l'Agora, *Aspects de la Jeune Photographie de Wallonie et de Bruxelles.* ¶ 1992 : Edinburgh (U-K), 369 Gallery, *I-D Nationale.* / Reims (F), Mai de la photo + Redu (B), *A'limage de rien.* / Brussels (B), Centre d'Art Contemporain, *Visages, paysages et autres rivages.* ¶ 1991 : Paris (F), Palais de Tokyo, Centre National de la Photographie, *La Photographie Belge.* / Namur (B), Maison de la Culture, *Photobiographies, Deuil et Mémoire.* / Bruxelles (B), Université Libre de Bruxelles, *Le Réel Distancié.* ¶ 1989 : New York (U.S.A), Marcuse Peiffer Gallery, *Contemporary Belgian Photography.* ¶ 1988 : Charleroi (B), Musée de la Photographie, *Photographie Ouverte.* / Brussels (B), Espace Photographique Contretype, *Imagine.* / 1987 : Liege (B), Espace 375, *Mois de la Photo.*
COMMISSIONS : ¶ 1999 : Brussels, *B 8,* photographic assignments carried out by Espace Photographique Contretype. ¶ 1997 : Quebec (CND), *Trois fois Trois paysages,* photographic assignments carried out by Centre VU. ¶ 1994-95 : *La ville et son cliché,* photographic assignments carried out by Espace Photographique Contretype, Saint-Gervais Photographie, Pro Helvetia et la Documentation Photographique de la Ville de Genève. / *Train & création,* commissioned by Peuple et Culture en Wallonie et à Bruxelles. ¶ 1993 : *Zinc, épreuves d'artistes,* commissioned by société Vieille-Montagne, Paris. ¶ 1991 : *Les déchets*

nucléaires, commissioned by l'O.N.D.R.A.F., Brussels.
TV APPEARANCES : ¶ *À l'image de rien,* produced by Richard Wandel for « Cargo de nuit », R.T.B.F., mai 92. ¶ « André Jasinski », produced by André Chandelle for « Cargo de nuit », R.T.B.F., avril 89.
FILMS : *Heur,* 16 mm N/B, 30 min., 1990.
PUBLICATIONS (SELECTION) : 1999 : *B 8,* Éditions Contretype et La Lettre Volée, Brussels (B) ¶ 1999 : *Le souci du document,* Vox Editions et Les 400 coups, Montreal (Canada). Text by Jennifer Couëlle. ¶ 1999 : *Un souffle d'air et de lumière,* Le Salon d'Art Editions, Brussels (B). Text by Daniel Desmedt. ¶ 1998 : *Trois fois Trois paysages,* VU Editions, Quebec (Canada). Text by Daniel Desmedt. ¶ 1996 : *CV photo,* review n°37 Winter 96 (Canada). Text by Jennifer Couëlle ¶ 1995 : *La ville et son cliché,* book co-edited by Contretype (B), Saint-Gervais Photographie, Pro Helvetia and Documentation Photographique-Ville de Genève (CH). *Katalog,* review March 95 (DK). Text by Alexandre Vanautgaerden. ¶ 1994 : *Tradition and the Unpredictable,* Museum of Fine Arts, Houston (U.S.A.) ¶ 1992 : *Primavera Fotografica 92,* General catalogue, Barcelona (E). Text by Jean Arrouye.

BENOÎT FONDU

THE ARCHITECT : A landscape architect trained at Gembloux and in London, Benoît Fondu feels that he is primarily a gardener. A keen botanist, he has been planning gardens in Belgium, England, France, Germany and Switzerland for about fifteen years. His enthusiasm for restoring historical gardens encouraged him to train as a landscape architect in Great Britain and subsequently work in that country before returning to the continent: he is presently in charge of the re-landscaping of the park of the Château de Seneffe (18th century). Aware of art and its place in nature and gardens, he likes to design areas, which are in harmony with their works of art.
DESCRIPTION : the work of the landscape gardener, besides providing technical assistance to the artists, can be seen in the general layout of the space, and more particularly in the drawing of leaf-shaped flower beds : Salix fragilis (Willow), Castanea sativa (Chestnut), Tilia americana (Lime), Carpinus betulus (Hornbeam). In the area of the « Garden of Maladies » laid out by René Pechère (1987), he introduced a yew-tree hedge in order to give dynamics to the perspective of Charles Van Elst's path (1932.) By doing away with the thickets which lined the surrounding wall, he could retake possession of the orchard area and emphasise this wall which appears today as a second enclosure after the first one which marks the boundary of the « Garden of Maladies. » Paths were covered with wood chips so as to lessen the harshness of earlier dolomite paths.
FLOWER BEDS' SIZE : Salix fragilis : 4,14 m (B.) x 0,68 m (L.) x 0,17 m (H.) ; Castanea sativa : 4,42 m (B.) x 1,04 m (L.) 0,17 m (H.) ; Tilia americana : 3,85 m (B.) x 2,26 m (L.) 0,17 m (H.) ; Carpinus betulus : 1,93 m (B.) x 0,91 m (L.) x 0,17 m (H.).
MATERIAL : Steel sheet.
TEAM : Els Claes, landscape architect ¶ Geert Flamand, horticultural engineer ¶ Dr. Andrew Sclater, historian and garden archaeologist ¶ Dominique Guerrier Dubarle, agricultural and horticultural engineer, Dip. CEAA « Historical Gardens and Landscape » (Versailles) ¶ Mieke Belien, agricultural and horticultural engineer, industrial designer, CAD. ADVISERS : Dominique Duchêne, forestry engineer ¶ Sandrine Godefroid, biologist, studies in flora ¶ Luc Schoonbaert, ornithologist ¶ Sim van Erwegen, arboriculturist ¶ J.P. Bauvin, horticultural engineer and teacher ¶ D. Huart, horticultural engineer, specialist in water ecology.
PARKS AND OPEN SPACES :
BELGIUM : ¶ **Chevetogne,** provincial park Valery Cousin, Province of Namur, 550 ha. [carrying out main plans for the re-evaluation of the park. Inventory and mapping of the important trees. Carrying out of various works, and presently engaged on the Esplanade] ¶ **Château de Seneffe,** Province of Hainaut, 28 ha. XVIIIth century park [inventory and mapping of important trees. Overall project. Mapping of present state of affairs in the park and making of a report of the development of the landscape. Complete restoration of : Orangery Gardens, the theatre, driveways, car parks, pool, avairy...] ¶ **Prieuré d'Anseremme,** Anseremme, Province of Namur [design and carrying out of work on the

Adage 501
SÆPE ETIAM EST OLITOR VALDE OPPORTUNA LOCUTUS
Even the gardener often makes opportunes remarks

park.] ¶ **Hôtel de Gaiffier d'Hestroy,** Namur, Province of Namur [study under way.] ¶ **Scy,** Province of Namur, 30 ha. [design and carrying out of work on new park on an old site. Complete refurbishment, access routes, tree planting, ponds. Building of « follies. »] ¶ **Province of Namur** [advisory work for the communes of the province of Namur.] ¶ **Archaeological Museum of South-East Flanders,** Velzeke, Province of East Flanders [advisory work on the construction of a Roman garden.] ¶ **Zoerselhof,** Province of Antwerp, 17 ha. Château with XVIIIth century atmosphere on an ancient Cistercien site. Contemporary sculpture Park [audit of tree stock laying out borders and flower beds. Stabilisation of banks. Restoration of XIXth century factory.] ¶ **Keerbergen,** Province of Brabant, 5 ha. Modern garden [restoration of plantations and structures : swimming pools, pathways, lighting.] ¶ **Het Looy,** Rijkevorsel, Province of Antwerp, 5 ha. Château of the end of the XIXth century. Contemporary sculpture Park [laying out of a new park on site of earlier plantings.] ¶ **De Bergen,** Asse, Province of Brabant, 17 ha. Château of the end of the XIXth century [laying out of a new park with lakes.] ¶ **La Hulpe,** Province of Brabant, 50 ha. [refurbishment of driveway, plantings. Laying out of park.] ¶ **Château du Chenoy,** Court St. Etienne, Province of Brabant. ¶ **Le Site de Silos de la Dendre,** Ath, Province of Hainaut [study in progress.] ¶ **Abbaye de Villers-la-Ville,** Province of Brabant [study in progress.]

ENGLAND : ¶ **Aswarby,** Sussex [project for an old park.] ¶ **Batsford Park,** Glos [historical resaerch and studies for the restoration of an important botanical collection, English Heritage.] ¶ **The Batsford Foundation,** site of a formal park of the XVIIIth century [historical study and maintenance study of contemporary arboretum and of japanese garden of the XIXth century.] ¶ **Borde Hill,** Sussex [historical research and restoration study of a botanical collection, English Heritage.] ¶ **Brighton Pavilion,** Sussex [historical research and restoration study for a Regency garden, English Heritage.] ¶ **Charleston Manor,** Sussex [historical research and restoration study for a formal garden designed by Walter Godfrey, P. Kandiah, Esq.] ¶ **Cirencester Park,** Glos [restoration study for an agricultural park of the XVIIIth century, English Heritage.] ¶ **Firle Park and Pleasure Grounds,** Sussex [restoration study for a XVIIIth century park, part of which was designed by William Emes, the Viscount Gage.] ¶ **Glynde Place,** Sussex [restoration study, English Heritage.] ¶ **Graveyte Manor,** Sussex [conseils techniques, English Heritage.] ¶ **Nymans,** Sussex [restoration research and study for one of the most important gardens of the National Trust, English Heritage.] ¶ **Old Campden House,** Glos [restoration research and study for a a XVIIth century garden, English Heritage.] ¶ **Wakehurst Place,** Sussex [restoration research and study for the botanical collection cared for by the Royal Botanic Gardens, Kew, for English Heritage.]

SCOTLAND : **Brodick Castle and Country Park,** Isle of Aran (National Trust for Scotland). **Culzean Castle and Country Park,** Ayrshire (National Trust for Scotland).

WALES : **Hafod,** Ceredigion [conservation strategy plan, Welsh Historic Gardens Trust.]

FRANCE : **Château du Nozet,** Pouilly-sur-Loire, Nièvre [rehabilitation of a project of the lanscape architect Duchêne, laying out of new areas in the park, aesthetic file and assessment of park. Refurbishment of vineyards, ponds, water management.] **Le Vieux Château,** Pouilly -sur-Loire, Nièvre [refurbishment of swimming pool and garden.] **La Poussie,** Sancerre, Cher [refurbishment of vineyard landscape, means of access.] **Avenue Victor Hugo,** Paris [refurbishment of garden for a company.] **Maison Pic Ier,** Chablis [refurbishment of entrance courtyard.]

SWISS : **Blonay,** Canton de Vevey [private garden]

GERMANY : **Ambassador's residence,** Berlin [refurbishment of a garden.] Belgian **Embassy,** Berlin [refurbishment of a garden.]

BIBLIOGRAPHY : *The Gardens of Europe,* in collaboration with Penelope Hobhouse and Patrick Tayler [translated into French, Dutch and German] / Russell Page, *Ritratti di giardini italiani,* study for a catalogue of an axhibition organised by the American Academy in Rome / *David Nash,* Parc Tournay-Solvay / Articles in *Les Cahiers de l'Urbanisme.*

GEORGES MEES

THE BOTANIST : A keen observer of the living world in all its most varied forms, Georges Mees first gained a degree in botanical science before a doctorate in veterinary medicine. His main areas of interest and research are focussed on Belgian flora, museum collections relating to veterinary science and the history of veterinary science: he is a founding member of A.E.F. (Amicale Européene de Floristique). He is also a founding member of the a.s.b.l. (a registered charity in Belgian Law), La Mémoire de l'Ecole Vétérinaire de Cureghem, set up to protect the historical and technical heritage of veterinary science as well as for the setting up of a project to establish a museum on the site of the veterinary school. At the same time he continues his activities in the subject of botany.

PUBLICATIONS (SELECTION) : ¶ 1958 : *Aperçu Phytosociologique sur la Vallée de la Semois,* thesis, Science Faculty, Department of Systematic Biology and of Phytogeography, Université Libre de Bruxelles, « Etude pharmacologique de l'Acide p-butoxyphényl–acéthydroxamique (CP 1044 J3) I. Propriétés pharmacodynamiques », *Medicina et Pharmacologia Experimentalis,* 15, *1966,* p. 307-321 ¶ 1966 : « Arylacethydroxamic Acids : A new Class of potent non-steroïd anti–inflamatory and analgesic Substances », *Nature,* 311, p. 752 ¶ Member of the editorial committee, and numerous publications in *Annales de Médecine vétérinaire,* Université de Liège, de 1976 à 1994 : « Benzodiazépines et Désinhibition (Recouvrement temporaire de l'Appétit) chez le Chat », *Annales de Médecine vétérinaire,* 126, 1982, p. 371-372 ¶ « La Journée du Patrimoine à la Faculté de Médecine vétérinaire à Cureghem », *Annales de Médecine vétérinaire,* 135, 1991, p. 317-337 ¶ Publications in the quarterly bulletin *Parcs Nationaux,* of the Association Ardenne et Gaume, 1976, 1978, 1979 ¶ « La Géologie de l'Ardenne : bref aperçu historique », *De la Meuse à l'Ardenne n°9,* 1989 ¶ « L'Hippiatrie ou la médecine du cheval à travers les âges », with G. Theves, L. Lassoie, a series of articles have appeared in *Veterinaria* and *Anderlechtensia,* bulletin of Cercle d'archéologie, folklore et d'histoire d'Anderlecht 1994-1997 ¶ « Étude morphométrique des squelettes équins mérovingiens de Tournai », with A. Gabriel, B. Collin, in *Actes du colloque d'histoire des connaissances zoologiques,* 6, journée d'études de l'Université de Liège : *Le cheval et autres équidés : aspects de l'histoire de leur insertion dans les activités humaines,* 12 mars 1994 ¶ « L'Ardenne, berceau du cheval ardennais », *Parcs et Réserves, vol.* 54, fascicule 1, janvier-mars 1999, p. 18 /27 ¶ Founding member of the a.s.b.l. (charitable foundation) Amicale européenne de floristique : A.E.F. member of the reading committee, numerous publications in the review *Adoxa* ¶ Publications in the quarterly review of the S.V.P.A., société pour la protection animale, 1999 ¶ *Le grand livre de la Forêt Wallonne,* avec P. Blerot, J-P. Lambot (éditeur), Mardaga, Liège, Bruxelles 1985 ¶ *De l'Art à la Science, ou 150 Ans de Médecine vétérinaire à Cureghem-Bruxelles,* avec P-P. Pastoret, M. Mammerickx, Éd. Annales de Médecine vétérinaire, 1986 ¶ *Les fouilles du quartier Saint-Brice à Tournai* 2, Université de Louvain, R. Brulet éditeur, Louvain-la-Neuve, 1991 ¶ *Le cheval ardennais,* avec P-P. Pastoret et al., Éditeurs du Point Vétérinaire, Maisons-Alfort, 1996.

EXHIBITIONS : ¶ 1986 : « Ecole Vétérinaire », on the occasion of its 150th anniversary, Cureghem, Brussels ¶ 1991 et 1994-1999 : Exhibitions and cultural gatherings as part of the programme of *Journées du Patrimoine* (Heritage Days) and on the departure of the Faculty of Veterinary Medicine ¶ 1993 : « L'Hippiatrie », Centre culturel de Vresse-sur-Semois, Ardennes ¶ 1993 : « L'Hippiatrie », Caves de Cureghem ¶ 1994 : setting up of the first rooms of the future Museum of Veterinary Medicine ¶ 1997 : Concept of the « Jardin d'Érasme », Musée de Saint-Antoine l'Abbaye, in collaboration with A. Vanautgaerden / Exhibited in the exhibition in honour of L. Willems, at the Genevermuseum, Hasselt.

Adage 4084
DOCEAT, QUI DIDICIT
He who was learned should teach

Alexandre Vanautgaerden

Adage 687
Tecum habita
Live with yourself

THE CURATOR : Art historian by training, Alexandre Vanautgaerden taught his subject and took part in numerous seminars on landscape before becoming curator of the museum in 1994. In parallel to his various research projects that led him to publish translations and studies on humanism, he has been the join producer of a number of films about contemporary artists. For four years he worked at the R.T.B.F. (a French-speaking, Belgian, public television) as a cultural editor. At the «Erasmus House Museum» he has developed a publications policy in co-operation with the publishing house «La lettre volée». In addition, a policy welcoming a number of foreign artists from different disciplines (dance, litterature, and visual arts) has been initiated. The project of laying out a philosophical garden resulted from the exhibition « Erasmus or the Praise of Curiosity in the Renaissance » and the creation of a temporary garden at the Musée de Saint-Antoine l'Abbaye in France in 1997. He is preparing, with Marie-Elisabeth Boutroue (I.R.H.T., C.N.R.S., Paris), an exhibition on colour and plant names and with Dr. Onghena, an exhibition on the theme of Vanity.

PUBLICATIONS (SELECTION) : ¶ 1991 : « Paysages en vue », in *04° 50', La mission photographique à Bruxelles, Bruxelles,* Édition Contretype & Région de Bruxelles-Capitale. / « Ombres dans un jardin en 'pourtaict' », in *Art public. Lieux publics, Bruxelles,* Communauté française - Fondation Roi Baudoin - La Papeterie. / « Meurtres dans un jardin public. A propos de Nicolas Schöffer », in *État des lieux. Art public. Lieux publics,* Bruxelles, Communauté française - Fondation Roi Baudoin - La Papeterie. / « Perejaume, l'oeil ne perçoit rien de certain », in *Arte Factum,* 38'91, avril-mai. ¶ 1992 : « Nils Udo / Bob Verschueren. Avec arbres et feuilles », *Arte Factum,* décembre 92/janvier 93, vol 10, n° 46. / « De schriftuur van Anne Denis », in *Engram* (Anne Denis, Thomas Lenden, Stephen Sack), de Gele Zaal, 27 november 1992 tot 9 januari 1993. / cat. *Laurent-Benoît Dewez (1731-1812), Christian Claus (1946), Anne Denis (1965)...dans les caves,* Édition Centre d'art contemporain du Luxembourg belge, Orval, Exposition juillet-août. / « À l'image de rien », in *Catalogue du Mai de la photo,* Reims. / « Félix Hannaert, le 8 juillet 1991 », in catalogue *Félix Hannaert,* Fondation pour l'Art belge contemporain, Bruxelles. ¶ 1993 : « 'Faire et ce faisant se faire' ou les malheurs de la peinture en cette fin de millénaire », in Art & Culture, octobre / *Répéter pour ne plus se divertir. Notes concernant un propos pascalien dans l'oeuvre de Luc Claus,* Alost. / « Fastenaekens, roman, in La Recherche photographique », Maison européenne de la photographie - Paris Audiovisuel - Paris VIII, Juin, n° 14. / « Années 80 : l'art en Belgique », in *L'annuel de l'Art,* mars-août. / « Barbara & Michaël Leisgen », in *Revue Contretype,* janvier - février, n° 36. ¶ 1994 : « Jean-Paul Brohez : 'Temps mort' », in *Revue Contretype.* / Notices pour *Le dictionnaire des peintres belges du XIV siècle à nos jours,* préface de Eliane De Wilde, Bruxelles, La Renaissance du Livre. ¶ 1995 : « « 'Faire et, ce faisant, se faire' ou comment la Maison d'Érasme est devenue le Musée Érasme », in *Miscellanea Jean-Pierre Vanden Branden : Erasmus ab Anderlaco,* Bruxelles, Archives et Bibliothèques de Belgique, Numéro spécial 49, pp. 21-51. / « Jean-Paul Brohez », in *Revue Contretype.* / « Photographier pour découper la nuit (à propos d'André Jasinski) », Katalog [en anglais et en danois.] ¶ 1997 : « Les éditions anciennes de 'l'Encomium medicinæ' », in Érasme, *L'Éloge de la médecine,* Tournai, Labor. / *Érasme ou l'Éloge de la curiosité à la Renaissance : Cabinets de curiosités et jardins de simples,* A. Vanautgaerden (s.l.d.), Bruxelles, La Lettre Volée à la Maison d'Érasme. / « Le grammairien, l'imprimeur et le sycophante ou Comment éditer une querelle théologique en 1520 [Érasme et Lee] », in *Érasme, Apologie d'Érasme ... qui lui servira de réponse aux deux invectives d'Edouard Lee...,* éd. A. Vanautgaerden, Bruxelles, La Lettre Volée, coll. Notulæ Erasmianæ, vol. I (Les Invectives), pp. 9-32. / En coll. avec Georges Mees, « Le jardin d'Érasme », in *Érasme ou l'Éloge de la curiosité à la Renaissance,* pp. 72-95. ¶ 1998 : « Érasme ou les muses rendormies », in *Éloge de l'Angleterre,* A. Vanautgaerden (s.l.d.), pp. 9–16, Bruxelles, La Lettre Volée, coll. Notulæ Erasmianæ, vol. II. / Avec Alain Van Dievoet, traduction de l'*Ode d'Érasme de Rotterdam pour dire les mérites de l'Angleterre,* ibidem. ¶ 1999 : « Vivre Bruxelles, sans l'art public », in *Art et architecture publics,* Yves Jacqmin (s.l.d.), Bruxelles, Région de Bruxelles-Capitale et Mardaga, pp. 147-152 / « Érika Rummel, Les 'Colloques' d'Érasme : Renouveau spirituel et

Réforme », *Moreana*, Mars, vol. 36, n° 137, pp. 111-114. ¶ 2000 : ' 'Érasme nègre' : l'Encomium medicinæ'. Histoire d'un texte et de ses éditions conservées à Bruxelles dans la Bibliothèque royale Albert Ier et au musée de la Maison d'Érasme », in *E Codibus Impressique. Opstellen voor Elly Cockx-Indestege*, Louvain, Peeters. / *Un premier jardin*, La Lettre volée à la Maison d'Érasme. / *L'homme qui tombait des étoiles*, La Lettre volée à la Maison d'Érasme.

TELEVISION (SELECTION) : Émission Intérieur Nuit, Cellule de production Cargo, R.T.B.F. (Télévision publique belge)

Diffusion hebdomadaire : R.T.B.F,. TV 5 Europe, Arte 21. Responsable de rubrique des séquences suivantes, réalisateur Richard Wandel (première diffusion) : Bob Verschueren (11/10/92) ¶ Joan Marti (10/01/93) ¶ Henri Van Lier (07/03/93) ¶ Tom Frantzen (09/05/93) ¶ Jacques Lizène (23/05/93) ¶ David Wicress, Paul Jaquette & Carole Jouffroy (31/10/93) ¶ Patricia et Marie-France Martin (03/01/94) ¶ Eric Sleichim/Blindman Quartet (13/03/94) ¶ Marie-Françoise Plissart (13/03/94) ¶ Pierre Van Steene (03/04/94) ¶ John Makepeace (25/09/94) ¶ « La partie d'Echecs » de Yves Hanchar (16/10/94) ¶ La bibliothèque de Marc-Henri Wajnberg (13/11/94) ¶ La bibliothèque de Beverly Joe Scott (11/12/94) ¶ Lenn Shelley (15/01/95) ¶ La bibliothèque de Colette Braeckman (12/02/95) ¶ Yves Bernard (26/0/95) ¶ La bibliothèque de Juan d'Oultremont (30/04/95) ¶ Hamadi (29/10/95) ¶ France Borel (07/01/96)

RESPONSABLE DES SÉQUENCES « IMAGE » SUIVANTES (première diffusion) : Daniel Brunemer (04/10/92) ¶ Marcel Broodthaers/James Ensor (11/10/92) ¶ La callandre Rolls Royce (31/10/92) ¶ Paul Jaquette (05/01/93) ¶ Dominique Thiolat/Marcelin Pleynet [L'amour vénitien] (24/01/93) ¶ René Magritte (31/01/93) ¶ Raymond Depardon (07/02/93) ¶ Edward Hopper ((11/04/93) ¶ Les palissades du quartier Léopold (18/04/93) ¶ Paul-Armand Gette ¶ Pierres de rêves chinoises (02/05/93) ¶ Marc Trivier (09/05/93) ¶ Robert Adams (16/05/93) ¶ Niele Toroni (23/05/93) ¶ Jean-Pascal Imsand (26/06/93) ¶ Pat Andréa (03/10/93) ¶ Dirck Braeckman (10/10/93) ¶ Ralph-Eugène Meatyard (17/10/93) ¶ Per Kirkebi (07/11/93) ¶ Estixtu Garcia (31/10/93) ¶ Walter Benjamin / Sarkis (03/01/94) ¶ Michaël Jackson (09/01/94) ¶ Hippiatrie (16/01/94) ¶ Guy Scarpetta (29/01/94) ¶ Gilbert Fastenaekens (06/02/94) ¶ Georges Meurant (13/02/94) ¶ Alain Buttard/Anne Denis (27/02/94) ¶ A. Serrano (06/03/94) ¶ Laetitia Yheap (13/03/94) ¶ Jean-Luc Dehaene (10/04/94) ¶ Félix Valloton (17/04/94) ¶ Marc Trivier (24/04/94) ¶ Liliane Vertessen (05/94) ¶ Le journal « De Morgen » (18/09/94) ¶ Jacques Vilet (09/94) ¶ Ann Mendelbaum (16/10/94) ¶ La peste en Inde raconté par le journal « Le Soir » (30/10/94) ¶ Les Minguettes (13/11/94) ¶ Zgorecki (27/11/94) ¶ John Vink (11/12/94) ¶ Gilbert Fastenaekens (01/01/95) ¶ *Family of man* (26/02/95) ¶ Nicole Dacos et les *Fiamminghi* (09/04/95) ¶ Pat Andrea (30/04/95) ¶ Jean-Paul Brohez (14/05/95) ¶ Échographies (27/09/95) ¶ Edouard Manet et Portman (07/01/96) ¶ La fuite du paysage (1996).

ÉMISSION ALICE, Cellule de production Cargo, R.T.B.F. : coréalisation, avec Wilbur Leguebe, de l'émission consacrée aux modifications urbanistiques à Bruxelles depuis l'expo 58, 14', première diffusion : Télé 21, septembre 1992.

VIDEOGRAPHY (SELECTION) : coréalisation avec Bernard De Wil pour l'image et Todor Todoroff pour les musiques originales : ¶ *Perejaume-Lied,* Prod. Les Arts Florissants & Centre Multimedia (Bruxelles), 8', 1990. ¶ *MUHKA* (Musée d'art contemporain d'Anvers), Prod. Lu Van Orschoven & Les Arts Florissants, 22', 1990-1991. ¶ *Faire un tableau...* [à propos de l'oeuvre de Madeleine Martin-Haupert], Prod. Les Arts Florissants & Padimunu, 57', 1993. ¶ *Des ombres...* [Marie-jo Lafontaine], Prod. Les Arts Florissants & Padimunu, 26', 1994. ¶ Une « Fiamminga » à Rome » [Nicole Dacos], Prod. Le Musée de la Maison d'Érasme, le C.P.C. & Les Arts Florissants, 24', 1995.

Opera omnia Desiderii Erasmi Roterodami, Basel, H. Frobenius & N. Episcopius, 1539-1542, collections of the Erasmus House, Museum, Paul Louis, 1997.

BIBLIOGRAPHY

Opera omnia Erasmi

Opera Omnia Des. Erasmi Roterodami, ed. Ioannes Clericus, Lugdunum Batavorum, 1703-1706.
Opera Omnia Desiderii Erasmi Roterodami, Amsterdam, North-Holland Publishing Company, 1969- (= ASD).
Collected Works of Erasmus, Toronto-Buffalo-Londres, Toronto University Press, 1974- (= CWE).

Opera selecta

Erasmo, *Obras escogidas*, Aguilar, S.A. de Ediciones, 1964
Erasmus von Rotterdam, *Ausgewählte Schriften*, ed. Wendelin Schmidt-Dengler, Darmstadt, Wissenschaftliche Buchgesellschaft, 1995 (1975)
Érasme, *Œuvres choisies*, éd. J. Chomarat, Paris, Le Livre de Poche, 1991.
Érasme, *Œuvres choisies*, éd. C. Blum, A. Godin, J.-Cl. Margolin, D. Ménager, Paris, R. Laffont, 1992.

Opus epistolarum Erasmi

Opus Epistolarum Desiderii Erasmi Roterodami, ed. P. S. Allen, 12 vol., Oxford, 1906-1965.
La Correspondance d'Érasme, Aloïs Gerlo (s.l.d.), 12 vol., Bruxelles, Institut pour l'Étude de la Renaissance et de l'Humanisme, 1967-1984.
The Correspondence of Erasmus, in CWE, vol. 1-11, 1974-1994.
Brieven van Erasmus, Antwerpen/Brussel/Gent/Louvain, Gilbert Degroote, 1985.
Erasmus in de spiegel van zijn brieven : een keuze uit de brieven van Erasmus, ed. O. Noordenbos en Truus van Leeuwen, Rotterdam, W.L. & J. Brusse's uitgeversmaatschappij, 1936.

Convivium religiosvm

Conuiuium religiosum, in *ASD*, vol. 1-3, ed. L.-E. Halkin, R. Hoven, F. Bierlaire, 1972.
Le banquet religieux, in *Cinq banquets*, J. Chomarat et D. Ménager (s.l.d.), Paris, Vrin, 1981
The Godly Feast, ed. Craigh R. Thompson, in *CWE*, vol. 39, 1997.
Het religieuze banket, in *Een derde twaalftal samenspraken*, C. Sobry, Antwerpen, De Sikkel, 1936

Franz Bierlaire, *Les « Colloques » d'Érasme : réforme des études, réforme des mœurs et réforme de l'Église au XVIe siècle*, Paris, Les Belles Lettres, 1978.

Hortus Erasmi

Jochen Becker, « 'Non est muta rerum natura' : die anschauliche Sittenlehre von Erasmus' Convivium religiosum », in *Ikonographie der Bibliotheken, Vortäge eines bibliotheks-historischen Seminars vom 13. bis 14. September in der Herzog August Bibliothek*, hsg. von Carsten-Pete Warncke, Wiesbaden, 1992, pp. 43-106.
Lucy L.E. Schlüter, *Niet alleen. Een kunsthistorische-etische plaatsbepaling van tuin en huis in het « Convivium religiosum » van Erasmus*, Amsterdam, Amsterdam University Press, 1995.
Alexandre Vanautgaerden (s.l.d.), *Érasme ou l'Éloge de la curiosité à la Renaissance: cabinets de curiosités et jardins de simples*, Bruxelles et Saint-Antoine l'Abbaye, La Lettre volée et le Musée de Saint-Antoine l'Abbaye, 1997.

Botanica

Otto Brunfels, *Herbarium vivæ icones*, Argentorati, I. Schottus, 1537
Leonard Fuchs, *De historia stirpium*, Basileæ, M. Isingrinus, 1542
Carolus Clusius, *Rariorum plantarum historia*, Antverpiæ, C. Plantinus, 1576
Matthias de L'Obel & Pierre Pena, *Nova stirpium adversaria*, Antverpiæ, C. Plantinus, 1576
Matthias de L'Obel, *Plantarum seu stirpium icones*, Antverpiæ, C. Plantinus, 1581
Pedacius Dioscoride, *Opera omnia*, Francfurti, Andreas Welchel, Claudius Marnius et Ioan. Aubrius, 1598
Rembert Dodœns, *Cruydtboeck*, Antwerpen, I. vander Loe, 1554
Rembert Dodœns, *Histoire des plantes*, traduite par Charles de L'Escluse, Anvers, I. vander Loe, 1557
Rembert Dodœns, *Stirpium Historiæ Pemptades sex sive Libri XXX*, Antverpiæ, C. Plantinus, 1616
Conrad Gessner, *Catalogus plantarum latine, græce, germanice et gallice*, Tiguri, C. Froschauer, 1542
Pietro Andrea Mattioli, *Les commentaires sur les six livres des Simples de Pedacius Dioscoride Anazarbéen*, Lyon, Jean d'Ogerolles, 1566

Publications of the Erasmus House Museum

La Lettre volée
[Coll. Notulæ Erasmianæ]
- VOL. I — *Apologie d'Érasme de Rotterdam... qui lui servira de réponse aux deux invectives d'Edouard Lee... précédée d'une invective d'Edouard Lee*, Alexandre Vanautgaerden (ed.), 1997.
- VOL. II — Érasme, *Éloge de l'Angleterre*, Jean-Claude Margolin et Alexandre Vanautgaerden (ed.), 1998.
- VOL. III — Érasme, *La Civilité puérile*, trad. et éd. Franz Bierlaire, 1999.

BE BEPUBLISHED:
- VOL. IV — Érasme, *Sur la vieillesse*, translated and edited by Jean-Claude Margolin, 2001.
- VOL. V — Érasme, *Spongia* et Ulrich von Hutten, *Expostulatio*, M. Samuel et A. Vanautgaerden (ed.).
- VOL. VI — Érasme, *La Vie de Thomas More*, translated and edited by Germain Marc'hadour.
- VOL. VII — Érasme, *La Vie de saint Jérôme*, translated and edited by André Godin.
- VOL. VIII — Érasme, *Apologie contre Alberto Pio*, translated and edited by Marie Theunissen-Faider.
- VOL. IX — Érasme, *La Paraphrase à l'Évangile selon saint Mathieu*, translated and edited by Guy Bedouelle.
- VOL. X — *Les Index des Adages*, Mihai Nasta et Alexandre Vanautgaerden (ed.).

[Coll. Le Cabinet d'Érasme]
- VOL I — *Érasme ou l'Éloge de la curiosité à la Renaissance: cabinets de curiosités et jardins de simples*, Alexandre Vanautgaerden (ed.), 1997.
- VOL II — *Hortus Erasmi*, Alexandre Vanautgaerden (ed.), 2000.

BE BEPUBLISHED:
- VOL III — Alexandre Vanautgaerden, *A philosophical Garden*, 2001.
- VOL IV — Alexandre Vanautgaerden, *The Man who fell the stars*, 2002.

[Coll. Lettres]
Hervé Le Tellier, *L'Orage en août. Érasme, Faust, Luther: une rencontre*, 1996.

Éditions du Scarabée
Olivier Smolders, *14 Adages d'Érasme*, ill. Michel Smolders, 1997.

Éditions Labor
Érasme, *Éloge de la médecine*, 1997.

Archives and Libraries of Belgium
Miscellanea Jean-Pierre Vanden Branden: Erasmus ab Anderlaco, André Van Rie (ed.), 1995.

PUBLISHED WITH THE SUPPORT OF

A.F.A.A., Association Française d'Action Artistique
(The Ministry of Foreign Affairs, France)
Anderlecht Commune
Pierre Hazette, Minister of Secondary Education,
Arts and Sciences for the « Communauté française » of Belgium
Intercommunale Bruxelloise de Distribution d'Eau (I.B.D.E.)
Vlaamse regering en Vlaams comité Keizer Karel 1500-2000
Bruxelles/Brussel 2000

SPONSORS

Arabel - Buchmann Optical Industries

WE WISH TO THANK THE FOLLOWING

Christian D'Hoogh, Mayor,
and Aldermen of the Commune of Anderlecht
who have supported this project with enthusiasm from the beginning

Annie Claise of Corning S.A. – Raymond Longin, teacher at Elishout School
and Fondation Roi Baudoin for its programme *École adopte un monument*
Geneviève François, Principal Advisor, General Delegation Wallonie-Bruxelles in Paris
Suzette Henrion, Director of the Department of plastic Arts, Ministry of the Communauté française of Belgium
Jacqueline Meido–Madiot, Advisor on Cultural Gatherings and Exhibitions
of the French Presidency of the European Union.

Alain Dierkens, Lecturer with special responsibility for cultural affairs (D.E.S.)
Université Libre of Brussels and the following trainees:
Aurore de Decker, Véronique Laheyne, Marie Naudin, Aurélie Meeus, Vincianne Picalause et Eve Toubeau

The personnel of the Public Works', Plantations' and Museums' Services who have made it possible to bring the
'Philosophical Garden' into existence.

André Delvaux, Alain Van Dievoet et Jozef Van den Broeck
who have given us constant support and guidance in our work

and

Henriette Mees
because Georges Mees, our botanist, doesn't have green fingers

The collection *Le cabinet d'Érasme*
is under the supervision of Alexandre Vanautgaerden,
Curator of the Erasmus House Museum.

All rights of translation, reproduction and adaptation
are reserved worldwide.
© Ante Post a.s.b.l. responsible for publications of « La Lettre volée »
20, boulevard Barthélemy, B - 1000 Bruxelles
& The Erasmus House Museum
31, rue du Chapitre, B - 1070 Bruxelles

Copyright : Bibliothèque Royale de Belgique
2nd Quarter 2001 - D/2001/5636/8
ISBN 2-87317-134-0

Typeset by [Sign'], Brussels,
in Foundry Old Style and Foundry Old Style Expert,
and printed on Phœnix (PB Paper) 135 grams
on the presses of Dereume, printers at Brussels, Spring 2001,